BENT LETTERS

Bent;

Twisted, crooked, warped, contorted, deformed, misshapen, out of shape, irregular – in regard to what is considered, "normal" or straight.

Letters;

a written, typed, or printed communication, especially one sent by mail or messenger, printed communications as legal or formal documents,

Why wouldn't it be God,

Who did you pray to,

and what did you pray?

If God can use me - then He can certainly use you!
ALL of us are important to Father and His Kingdom!
WE are all needed by Him.
Our walks, prayers, and obedience to the relationship
are important.
NEVER let go of your dreams and visions for Jesus!

Father's Hand Ministries
Neil W Gamble
8012 Scotia Rd. Newport, WA 99156

Dreams and visions seem to be a common way that the Lord communicates with people. Through all time, in the Word, we see Father using dreams and visions to guide people, bring answers to questions or prayers spoken to Him or to talk to them. In this book I relate some of those I have experienced that have had a profound impact on my walk. I do not look for them, nor do I believe all of my dreams and visions are from Father! I do test them and ponder them. If they are from God they will stand. A lot of revelations and the illumination of Father, Son and Holy Spirit, and my relationship to them, has come through the following spiritual encounters. **They are not theological nor meant to be.** They are part of God's continued communion and conversations with me.

I have been writing this book for about 5 years. I have deleted it, written it again and changed it repeatedly. I was struggling, but with my precious wife's continuous support and prodding, along with help from a few good friends, Father has seen me through! I pray the results of all this is worth something to Jesus and Father's Kingdom!

Neil W Gamble - In Father's Hand!

Table of Contents

Bent Letters;

I am a man given to dreams, visions, and spiritual experiences. I am a man dedicated to "know" the Father, Son, and Holy Spirit. I want to experience the book of Acts and life in the Spirit. I have sat with Father in "Heaven", stood before Jesus and Father in The Throne Room, and have had many spiritual encounters and kingdom manifestations concerning His purpose and love.

*My prayers tend to center on; "I want to 'know' you Jesus, I want to experience your heart and desires. Father, whatever it costs, takes or whatever needs to happen in my life to know you, so be it. I want to fulfill the desire of **Your** heart!"*

Even though that is my focus, at times I tend to be "a foot-dragging disciple!" Much of my life in Christ would appear "BENT" from a traditional Christian perspective. I just don't fit in the box marked "Christian" defined by denominational or conventional thought. I don't regularly attend "traditional church services" but I fellowship and pray with believers quite often!

I do not have a set prayer and devotion time, though I tend to have intimate times with Father and Jesus more often in the mornings around sunrise with a cup of coffee. I don't fast unless Jesus tells me to. Every day I spend my life with Jesus and my hours are filled with prayer that looks and sounds a lot like a conversation between friends. There are not a lot of "pious clichés" in our communion, but real, emotional, natural talk that most times deals with or is about others, the future, the past, His desires or direction. It is what I call responsive communion or prayer. I listen and He directs my words. (This kind of prayer is life changing). My wife Dana and I have fellowship at our home or other's houses often, and most days there seems to be a conversation that includes Jesus and His purpose going on every time we sit down or strike up a conversation.

Most days, I know some of what will happen as HS (Holy Spirit) "guides me into the truth and shows me things to come" (part of Jn.16:13). Some of what He shows me is profound and yet much of it just has to do with He and I and life. I have seen so many miracles, signs and wonders through the years, most of which happened outside the traditional church walls and meetings, (though we have had some profound traditional church meetings through the years).

Most people would probably define me as a rebel or at least a bit rebellious. I am OK with that. I am not out to be offensive or divisional in any way, but know that much of what I share is a bit outside the paradigm of acceptable or submissive to Sunday centered church order. I read a lot, but it is not a specific sit down and study desk time.

My days are filled with conversations with Jesus. I write down a lot of what we talk about, but it is not with a "I must do this" attitude, rather it is conversational writing, listening, and meditating as Holy Spirit leads.

Sometimes I will spend hours in the Word and listening to the Spirit, then write letters or documents as a result that I feel others might find interesting, motivational or controversial. My studies are focused on being approved of by God and knowing Him better. I seldom study to get sermons or preaching material. **I live for the audience of One**; then walk that out daily in my world with others the best I can.

"**Bent Letters**" is a compilation of that which came out of my studies or some type of spiritual experience, vision or encounter with Jesus that may have been written as stand-alone documents. I have gathered a few of them, edited and added to these basic Biblical principles with some thoughts and perspectives gotten through the years of trainings and teachings we have given around the world. It also includes some "Bent" experiences with God in the midst of living with Him! Looking at the New Testament and the practices of the people in the book of Acts, along with the rest of the written letters presented in the Word, I realized that we, the Church, have "bent" these scripture letters to have them agree with what we would like them to say. As for God's voice, whatever we would like to have Him say seems to be what we hear and then we tell others, "God said" or "thus saith the Lord."

Maybe it is time we quit "bending" His letters to suit our own wants and desires, and instead bring our traditions to Him and let us be "bent back" to His purpose and truth.

We, The Church of Christ, are to be an example of Christ to the lost. Our love (the God kind of naturally supernatural love – Agape') is to be seen in all we do.

God's love is our position with Him. He does not try to love us, but instead **IS** Love to us. Father loves by being who He is and having His focus be us. We are to be "like Him." (Jn.20:21-23)

There is a standard of conduct in God. Most of His kids want to live in the place of ignoring the reality of responsibility, honor, and obedience. He says, "the truth sets you free", thus there must be a place of bondage when the truth is not accepted and lived or before it encounters us. Abiding in the truth, being the truth, exhibiting the truth, is how we are to live and present Him to the world.

Ephesians 4:15 (AMPC) Rather, let our lives lovingly express truth [in all things, speaking truly, dealing truly, living truly]. Enfolded in love, let us grow up in every way and in all things into Him Who is the Head, [even] Christ (the Messiah, the Anointed One).

There is a responsibility to "knowing" Jesus! Most do not want to be responsible or accountable for their part in the relationship. They want everything to be 'free' – thus the problem, as there is no such relationship which costs nothing. The Word itself shows that there is a need of more than one party participating or giving into what is happening in God's Kingdom. If we are going to be *The*

Church Jesus is returning for, we may need to go back and look at our foundational teachings on many subjects that we now walk in and look at them from God's perspective. There are over 1500 "IF's" in the written Word connected with His promises to us.

Father has always wanted to show the world His love. **We are to be vessels that show Him.** Miracles have always and **will** always be a part of showing the world that "He is." He has endeavored from the beginning to make us a blessing to others, but we continue to bring the things He does around to it being all about us. His purpose is to seek and save the lost, destroy the works of the enemy (thus destroying the effect of sin) and to redeem man from our broken relationship with Him. Jesus demonstrated and modeled what the Gospel we are to share should look like; His presence **is** THE "naturally supernatural"! The apostles/disciples began the Church age with the miraculous, and Paul says that the Gospel is a demonstration of the Spirit and Power! <u>What Gospel do we bring, live or share?</u> Jesus' goal is bringing us back into a place of living with Father. His principles and direction will stand as "**<u>The Truth enfolded in (His naturally supernatural) Love.</u>**" (Eph. 4:15 AMPC) unto eternity. (*<u>Eternity is not time without end but a place without time</u>*). *The reason Jesus is in the midst of correcting His Church could be that we may have wrong thinking, which is when the traditions of men have more influence than His Word in our lives. We will choose our future, the future of "church" and shape the future of others with our decisions as we walk with Jesus, led by HS. These bent ramblings are simply "food for thought." Make your own conclusions.*

The Foundation of Truth;

Nowhere does it say you need certain qualifications (perfection or a high education) to "do the works of God." It is about being who we are. If we have received Jesus and He is Lord, then we are children of God! There are some major misconceptions that we have been traditionally taught. One of the greatest deceptions that the enemy has sold the Body of Christ is that only certain well-trained individuals can expect to see Father and Jesus move miraculously through Holy Spirit or can hear His voice clearly. The thought that my life is not "holy enough" for God to do miracles through my walk, and that my prayers are not spoken correctly so no miracles will happen, is such a lie. For me to believe that Father does not talk to me like He does with others is such a sham!

The greatest lie is the truth spoken at the right moment or in such a way that it leads us to the wrong conclusion or in the wrong direction! There are some aspects of my living that are important in my walk, but NO works or education will make me more worthy of Jesus' sacrifice for me! As a result of me accepting His amazing sacrifice, my life and walk is changed and run in a different direction than it did before; **because I am changed by His blood, and the resulting "New Covenant" I have received.**

Eve was tempted with the truth that she would die (be separated from the life of God and her position with Him), if she ate the fruit from the tree of the knowledge of good and evil. The truth was given to her as a question, in a way that caused her to question God's Love, character and integrity, and also who she was created to be.

Jesus, the son of man, was tempted with what was already His. The enemy tried to get Jesus to give allegiance to him to get the position that was His already and whom He was created for and to live by Father.

Today the "Church" is trying to "attain" the promises and position, the identity given by God to us. Rather than BE who we are, we have swallowed a lie that we must "work" to receive our position, and what is already ours. The enemy constantly tells us that what we have done in trying to prove who we are was not enough or done wrong or was in the wrong timing. _Deception, fear or disapproval are the enemy's favorite tools to use on us because they still work!_

W**e _tend to live in a place of insecurity where a lie seems more_**

 powerful than the truth! In this temporal arena we live in there will always be something physically, emotionally or spiritually that would destroy our trust in and adherence to Father and thus not live out our position in Him. The enemy is an opportunist and is always looking for what we might fall for to keep us from recognizing our identity or being who we are. Status in life, hierarchical position, our job or profession, and or our education do not change our name or our true identity!

Our relationship with Jesus does. Our choices will show who we trust and believe along with who we actually believe we are. Trust is the *action* of Faith and "Faith works by Love." Trust has to be seen. It shows as we obey. Christianity is "The Divine Person, His Love and Power" in action. It is Holy Spirit (HS) bringing life to the Word. Trust produces the witness of God through us.

I was in another country, and one of my duties on this trip was to teach a large group of denominational pastors and worship leaders about intimacy and discipleship. The first morning, before the meetings began, I was reading about David dancing before the arc and his wife being quite upset, and David's reply. "I will be even more undignified than this, and will be humble in my own sight..." (2 Sam.6:22). In the morning session I had laid a foundation for what I would be teaching for the next two days. After lunch I was in the back of the long narrow old church packed with about 400 leaders expecting this "anointed teacher" to teach them. As the host was giving more details of my credentials, (a flowery explanation about who I was and what I had done), God, through HS, spoke in my spirit and said, "If you will dance before me up the aisle I will follow."

These leaders did not even believe in the miraculous expression of Holy Spirit. I told God that I was a cowboy and dancing up the aisle would only create a lot of laughter and would make me look pretty dumb after my host had been so gracious with his introduction.

Holy Spirit's reply was, "Would you like to do something more undignified than dance?" Immediately I decided that dancing would be fine! So I started, and just like I had expected everyone started laughing.

Embarrassed, I told HS that it was just what I thought would happen, everyone was laughing. His reply, "Who are you dancing for?" At that moment, I lost sight of the people and no longer heard the laughter. I danced before my Lord down the aisle! When I got to the front and turned around a pastor jumped up, came over and dropped to his knees, and through tears and anguish cried out, "I am in sin, I am filled with lust, please pray for me!" In that moment of time everywhere in the building these leaders began repenting and weeping, crying out to God, confessing their sins to one another, getting healed, delivered and baptized in the Spirit. It was about 2 hours before the place quieted down — everyone was changed! I didn't speak, just stood, cried and watched as HS changed us all.

I have no idea how long it took me to dance down that aisle, but the results of my trust was transformation in a lot of lives. This meeting was about confirmation to those leaders that God was bigger than they could imagine. He was asking me to show faith and trust Him. I wonder what would have happened if I didn't "know" Him and His voice? We cannot experience HS and show no sign of it. Choice is always a key part of our trust and faith showing.

Finding a Solder Joint:

The first time I became really aware of Christ "guiding me into all truth" at work happened starting about 5 days after going to work in Boise ID. on the development of a new type of irrigation machine. I had to leave to go to California to repair a machine that I had never worked on or seen running 5 days after I was hired. My job was to be the field technician who made what the engineers in the development office came up with work in real life situations. I had seen the machine I was to work with one day at this point. I did not even know how to get this machine started, much less repair it! On the 14 hr trip down to Bakersfield area where this machine was, that no one could get running, I found myself praying in tongues continuously.

This machine was on a cotton field and had not run for a couple days. It had to run or the crop would be ruined. Neither the repair people nor the engineers that were there could get it to move. My new employer told me to get down there and fix it! I had been putting together tools and getting repair parts and blueprints organized in my new service vehicle as well as meeting with my new boss and other workers I would be around.

I had absolutely no knowledge of this machine. On the trip down from Boise to repair this machine, as you might imagine, I was praying constantly for Jesus to lend me a bit of help. I arrived very early on a Monday morning before anyone else so I could look at the machine and maybe see if I could fix it. I realized quickly I did not even know where to begin to look for the problem. So, I left and checked into my motel, took a quick shower, then ate. I arrived at the machine again right at 8 am as appointed. Three men were waiting for me, an engineer, a service tech, and the owner of the land. They looked on expectantly as I approached the machine, I stopped, introduced myself, then proceeded to open the two panels that operated the machine.

My thoughts as I opened the two doors, "Wow, so this is what the operating panels looks like." I actually laughed out loud as I realized the absurdity of me being there. One of the men asked, "What is so funny?" I smiled and responded, "Nothing." My laugh was about me fixing this thing I did not even know how to start. This whole situation had to be a joke as it was not possible! As I stood gazing into this panel, that I have no idea how to begin to fix, the Lord began to speak to me, "Look".

As a result of His word, I found myself focusing on one circuit board with a bunch of rows of circuits on it that all looked alike; in the control panel that was full of electronic relays and circuit boards. One of the electronics boards was about 2"x4" in size with about 20 or so rows of all these tiny triacs, diodes, etc. on each line exactly the same. As I continued to gaze at it wondering what was happening, Jesus put a magnifying lens on my eye, (that is the only way to describe what happened to me). As I looked, I could see each individual solder joint on each line of these electronic circuits. There was over a hundred joints, but my eye was focused on one joint and I could see that it was not soldered as it should have been. Careful not to look away in case I would not be able to find it again, I took a pen out of my pocket, reached in and put a small mark on the board by this bad joint. Without saying a word to those watching, I went back to my vehicle, got my brand-new soldering iron (that was still in its packaging), put the batteries in it, tinned the end of it with some solder in preparation for its first use and returned to the panel. In front of this panel there is only room for one person to stand so no one could see what I was doing. They were trying to figure out what was going on but I ignored them and proceeded to put a bit of solder on the bad joint I had seen through Jesus' magnifying glass.

I was in a zone with Jesus as He was giving me a understanding of what had happened a few times before this, that I had not comprehended.

Now He was talking to me and showing me how to do what was needed to get the machine running. Several scriptures were coming alive to me in a different way than I had been taught. Jn. 14:26, 15:26 and 16:13 were no longer about religious times or just scripture! This was about life, work, and helping me do my job and thus helping others.

Since I did not know how to operate this irrigation machine yet, and did not want them to know this, when I finished soldering the bad joint, I turned to the service tech that was watching and asked if he would go ahead and start the machine up while I went and put up my tools. By the time I got back to the machine it was up and running. It had taken me all of 15 minutes to get it repaired. They had been working on it for several days before I got there and had not been able to find the problem. Jesus is so cool! Since everything that is created was created by Him first, He knows how to fix or repair them! As we finished up we moved away from the irrigation machine and the guys who were there asked me how I knew where to look and what was wrong? Inside I was filled with laughter as I realized that Jesus had set me up. This was what my 14-hour drive and prayer time had been about - to be a witness! In response to their question I replied, "Do you really want to know?"

Knowing that what I was about to say would sound so ridiculous to these worldly men, I waited for them to answer.

"Of course, we want to know what you did. We will have to work on this machine in the future and we need to know how to repair it." "Ok, this is how I knew what to repair. For 14 hours driving here I prayed since I did not know anything about this machine. When I got here, I did not even know how to start it, had never seen all the controls, nor had I seen one run. As I opened the panel and was looking at the controls Jesus put a magnifying glass on my eye and I could see that one solder joint that was not soldered correctly on that one small electronic board. So, I did what He told me to and the machine is repaired"! The engineer laughed at me and walked away, the farmer cursed a bit then walked away, the repair technician looked at me and walked away. As I stood there in awe, I had such a wonderful peace and confidence settle in my spirit.

Jesus did not send me to have no one respond, one of these men would be back during the week I was to stay and watch this machine and learn about it. The next day the farmer and the technician both came to me and asked me more about what had happened. During that summer I made many trips to this machine and each time I showed up I was able to repair the machine quickly and as long as I was there it would run perfectly. These two who had responded to my story and I would have amazing talks about My Savior and Holy Spirit's guidance in all I do. The service tech gave his life to the Lord and the farmer admitted that he had known Jesus but had quit walking with Him some years back. He was restored to Jesus and we had some great scripture studies together. This event changed my whole view of what real Christianity should be like. It cemented a foundation in me of the need for all of His followers to hear His voice - not just a few leaders or special folks.

We are not to do works to get His approval. We are to do works as a result of hearing His voice and having an intimate relationship with Him. Jn. 20:21 says we are sent just like Him! It is one of many scriptures that contradict the teaching that we are less than He was as He walked this earth. Arrogance is not found in our saying and believing that we are to be just like Him, but it is found in discounting and walking contrary to His Word, our position and His purpose. We are not worms, nor are we given less that He had as He walked as a man among us.

That is NOT so according to His Word! Arrogance and pride put comfort, tradition and the needs of self above His provisions, precepts and His sacrifice, that restores us to being children of God again. I pray that this book moves you to be either glad, sad or mad, that it does not leave you the same. We need to be whom we were created to be. Jesus, as the second Adam demonstrates and reveals to us what man was made to be in the beginning.

He models the identity, perspective and position man was created live in as intimate sons and daughters of God.

Knowing Him;

I was ministering with a friend of mine in a small town in Idaho. We were experiencing the Lord's presence. HS was moving amongst the people and miracles were happening. It was a several day ministry and during the time we were not ministering we would find high points around the city to pray from. After a couple of meetings, we were pretty thrilled at what the Lord was doing. As we sat in my pickup on a hill praying over the city, my friend turned to me and said that the Lord had just spoken to him. He told him that he had worship down. He said that he could bring the people into His presence and move them to a place of openness through what he sang or played. "But," He said, "_You do not know Me!_" The moment my friend spoke, the Lord spoke to me, though a bit differently. "Neil, you can bring people to my throne and cause them to hear me. You preach well and can bring me to healing and compassion for those in our midst, *BUT, YOU DO NOT **KNOW** ME!"* These words so hit me that I was instantly broken! I knew right then that walking with Jesus was way more than "doing" ministry for Jesus. I do not remember the rest of the time in that town as I was consumed with Jesus' statement to me, "You do not Know me!" Once home, I began to search out this word "know," and my focus in life was radically changed.

To "know" in a relationship is to be close, intimate, and to have a deep understanding of the other party in the relationship. I found in the Hebrew origin of the Greek word for the word "know" that it is to be like a husband-and-wife relationship—vulnerable, entwined, emotionally connected, caring, dynamic and passionate. It is to be way more than just best friends. *(These previous definitions are words I came up with after my study of the word **know** and looking at the definitions I found and then putting them in my language).* As a result of this study, there are two passages of scripture that at times still hound me; Mt. 7:21-23 and Lu.13:22-27. It would be good if we do not avoid these passages in judging ourselves and our lives in Christ, least we be judged.

Mt. 7:21-23 (NKJV) "Not everyone who says to Me, 'Lord, Lord,' shall enter the kingdom of heaven, but he who does the will of My Father in heaven. Many will say to Me in that day, 'Lord, Lord, have we not prophesied in Your name, cast out demons in Your name, and done many wonders in Your name?' And then I will declare to them, 'I never knew you; depart from Me, you who practice lawlessness!"

Lu. 13:23-27 (NKJV). "Then one said to Him, "Lord, are there few who are saved?" And He said to them, "Strive to enter through the narrow gate, for many, I say to you, will seek to enter and will not be able. When once the Master of the house has risen up and shut the door, and you begin to stand outside and knock at the door, saying, 'Lord, Lord, open for us,' and He will answer and say to you, 'I do not know you, where you are from,' then you will begin to say, 'We ate and drank in Your presence, and You taught in our streets.'

But He will say, 'I tell you I do not know you, where you are from. Depart from Me, all you workers of iniquity." My continued studies of these two scriptures revealed to me that we can keep Jesus from "knowing us or being close to us" by **our** decisions not to be close to Him. Relationships are two-way streets. They are communication and communion, not a one-way conversation! *The cost of knowing Jesus is to be known by Him.* Let me put this in different words; there is a cost to being known and to know someone. That cost requires honor, obedience and sacrificial commitment. It is time spent pursuing a greater relationship, being vulnerable to the living God. To do this you must come to the place where you actually believe what scriptures say about Father, Son and Spirit. THEY are ALIVE! I can communicate, talk with, walk with, and understand them. It just takes vulnerability, surrender, and abandonment, time and a death to the importance of **self**.

Love, God's love, the foundation;

Agape' is defined as "God's Love." By definition it is an abundant moral or social love. In doing a study of His Word on this subject we find that charity or benevolence by someone with regard for others to be a common thought about agape'. It is Love that gives because **He is and has**, and there is a need of an action of His Love. Without the thought of what will be received back for doing or being what is needed, Father gives. (God **gave** His only begotten son – for us – without knowing whether we would respond to His demonstration of Love or not). <u>I believe that even that definition is too small for the reality of God's love.</u> **God is love -** <u>Thus the definition of Agape' is found in the whole of God's character and attributes totaled together.</u> Being Love compels one to do what is needed (in truth, righteousness and integrity) to create an opportunity for a relationship.

Love is self-contained yet isn't fulfilled without giving and being "love" to someone. Today, more than ever, I am convinced we do not have a complete understanding of the term Agape', "God's Love or God is love." that comes close to the reality of including all of His attributes and character.

Back in 1982 I was studying the term *Agape'* or "God's Love." I knew nothing about love as most of my life had been lived for me. I had finally made Jesus "My Lord" and submitted to His direction about a year or so before this. After my surrender to His pursuit of me, I could not get enough of His presence or His Word. I was hungry to know Him!

I found myself reading 1 Cor. 13:1-8 and 1 John 4:7-21 along with a few other passages about Love, but mainly these scriptures. I wanted to understand God, and the Word says that He is Love. I needed to find out what His love is as, "*who you are is a foundation for all you do.*" In other words, what you do reveals who you are in many ways. I was traveling a lot on the job I had at the time and being gone 2 weeks at a time was pretty normal. I carried several Bible reference books and a variety of bibles with me on my work journeys. I spent a lot of time in motels at night reading and pursuing the idea of knowing God. I had gotten "baptized in the

Holy Spirit" earlier that year and it had opened up a whole new world of revelation to me. As I re-read a lot of scripture that I had read before the "Spirit came upon me", I was blown away at what I began to see. (*The Word says that Holy Spirit "will guide you into all truth and show you things to come"*) (Jn.16:13) . On one such trip I was studying 1 Jn.4:17-19 (NKJV):

"Love has been perfected among us in this: that we may have boldness in the day of judgment; because as He is, so are we in this world. There is no fear in love; but perfect love casts out fear, because fear involves torment. But he who fears has not been made perfect in love. We love Him because He first loved us."

I had taken all the words in this scripture passage and looked up definitions for them and then re-wrote the verses using the definitions I had found.

I was talking with Jesus and Holy Spirit, listening, and attempting to understand this scripture passage; "perfect love casts out fear because fear involves torment. He who fears has not been made perfect in Love." I had been studying this passage for weeks and on this trip, I had been studying every moment I could while not working.

It was a Thursday evening, and I did not have anything to do until Monday, so I was having a marathon session with Jesus, Holy Spirit and the scripture. About 3-4 am Friday morning I had a revelation of God's love! It hit me like a big hammer. I found myself standing on my bed weeping and crying as God filled me with a life-changing revelation of the power of Love!

I was 600 miles away from my best friend and wife, Dana. It was 4 am and she had our two sons and life there so I couldn't call her at this early morning hour and expect a good reaction. My problem was that; ***When you have a revelation of perfect love, you have to share it! Love must be shared because it is LOVE!*** **Love's reality is only found in sharing or giving it away.**

A Fresh Revelation of Father's Love;
profound, but crazy!

Day 1: I was a bit overwhelmed, crying and begging God to give me someone to call at that hour of the morning in the town I was in, where I knew no one. I needed to share this revelation with someone! I was a mess, broken and undone, standing on my motel room bed in God's presence crying, "You must give me someone to share this revelation with". Then I hear God say, "Look up." I did and there in the middle of the ceiling was a black housefly. I replied, "See Lord, this is what I am talking about. I think I am going crazy with this revelation because I could swear I heard you say 'look up' and as I do, I think you are telling me to share Your "perfect love" with this fly on the ceiling". Ignoring the fly, I asked Him afresh, "please give me someone to share with. I cannot contain this Love I am experiencing"! For a second time I hear, "Look up" and "share My love with this fly." I now **knew** for sure that I was going crazy and let the Lord know my feelings once more. The fly remained on the ceiling, and I could not get away from the thought that Father was telling me to share His perfect love with this insect. Pondering my situation for a few moments in silence, brought a variety of possibilities to this dilemma I found myself experiencing. Either I was going crazy as I feared, or God had answered my request rather uniquely or there was another option that I had not thought of yet.   I sat down on the bed and stared at this fly on the ceiling wondering, "What if this is God?" The only way to find out if what I was trying to avoid was God, was to speak to the fly. I got up, checked the room, the window, and the door to make sure no one was listening to what was going on in my room. Then, I sat back down on the bed, and it began…   "OK fly, I promise not to hurt you in any way. I will not kill you either. Fly, land on my left hand." This fly immediately drops from the ceiling directly to my left hand! Ok, that is too easy I thought… and it could be a coincidence. So, I speak to it again, "Fly, land on my right hand." It instantly flies from my left hand to my right one. That is still too easy, "Fly, land on my nose." With no hesitation it moves to my nose and begins walking up and down the bridge of my nose making little buzzing noises with its wings.

You need to remember that at the heart of what is happening here are my prayers and my study of what it means to "know and be known by God." I was on a quest to know the Love of God!

<u>This experience seemed to be a direct response to my persistent, relentless pursuit of God and knowing His Love.</u>

For about a half hour or so I continued to test this unique experience of, "Perfect love sharing with a fly thing." I had the fly walk on the rim of my glasses, move to my bible that was open on the bed, move to my suitcase and rest on the handle, etc.... It obeyed everything I told it to do.

This had started about 3-4ish am. So around 5-6 AM or so, I tell the fly I must sleep for a while, and it needs to go back to the ceiling so I can. It left and I slept about 3 hours and when I awoke, the first thing I saw was this fly leaving the ceiling, landing on my nose, buzzing and walking up and down it! The fly seemed to desperately want to be close to me. I stayed in the room all that day, and the fly was in everything. I would try to read a passage and the fly would land on it and make buzzing sounds. I would try to write, and the fly would be on my pen or hand. I had on a long-sleeved shirt that day and at one point this fly goes inside my sleeve at my wrist and walks up my arm under my shirt and comes out at the neck of the shirt. Flies do not do that! By about 9 that night I was worn out with God's revelations of sharing perfect love to a fly! This insect had no fear of me in any way. It was unnerving! Whatever I told it to do, it did, and it constantly seemed to desire attention from me! I spoke to it, "Fly I must sleep, go to the ceiling, I am going to bed." It obeyed, I laughed thinking, "I am bent and over my head here" and went to sleep.

Day 2: I awoke to a fly landing on my nose making buzzing sounds. I was hungry so went out to have breakfast at a restaurant that was next to the motel. As I entered, three waitresses came and ALL of them wanted me to sit in their areas of service.

They started to argue about it! I told them that I would sit by the coffee pots so all of them could come by where I was. These women, whom I have never met before, came by my table and began to share their life stories with me. They shared their fears, sins, and problems with me.

They told me things I should not have ever known! I was so undone by these women being so honest with me that I just sat there listening nodding once in a while. I felt bad for the other patrons as they were focused on talking to me. I do not remember speaking to them, I had no clue what to say. I finally paid my bill and left. All three saw me to the door, gave me hugs and went back to work. I went back to my room, having forgotten about the fly, because of the experience with the waitresses. I opened the door, stepped in and the fly was instantly on my glasses buzzing! At about 7 pm or so I decided I needed a break from the Lord and this fly He was using as my example of what being perfect love looked like. I decided to go back to the restaurant and have supper. When I arrived two new waitresses fought over where I would sit and I again chose to sit by the coffee pots. There was a middle-aged man sitting at the counter on a stool watching me as I began to eat, while one of the waitresses was telling me her life stories, as had the ones at breakfast. Eventually, he gets up and comes to my booth and sat down without asking. After a moment or two he began to tell me about how badly he has treated his wife and family (not abusive but negligent). He explained that he did not know how to love anyone and that his life was all about him. It took him about an hour to unload his entire life story onto me. Again, I did not answer him or speak, I just listened. Two other men came and joined him at my booth, but did not say much.

I ended up praying over him, the waitresses and those other two guys before I left.   Back at the motel, I am beginning to get the idea that this is much bigger than "a fly." I was such a wreck by then that I simply wanted to sleep, so I showered and went to sleep ignoring the presence of the pesky fly.

Day 3: As I awoke, the fly landed on my nose again. This was so crazy! In a moment of time, I became so overwhelmed at God and His persistence in trying to get me to understand something that seemed beyond my abilities to comprehend or apprehend about His Love and presence. Using a fly was outside acceptable, yet here I was. This experience was beginning to weigh on me. I studied a bit but was hungry so went back to the restaurant. The three waitresses from the previous day were waiting for me; I sat at my "regular booth by the coffee," and they continued to stop and share their lives with me. The guy from the night before showed up and he joined me again without asking. Two hours later I excused myself from all of them and left. *I felt overwhelmed and had no way to understand the significance of all that was going on.* At the motel room waiting was my now constant companion - Mr. fly! The challenges in this revelation on God's Love and the events I was experiencing were taking a toll. God's love is in "being", not trying to do! Near the end of that 3rd day, the fly became increasingly pesky. The fly was on whatever page of the Bible that I was trying to read and was constantly making its buzzing noise attempting to distract me. The impossibility of this 3-day experience and the profound interaction with God, this fly, and the people in the restaurant deeply affected my identity and perspective of the word Agape'.

During the next couple of hours, Father brought me a whole new understanding of His Love and Him **being** Love. I had revelations about how important "compelled" obedience is as opposed to "demanded" obedience done by those who "say" they have faith in Him, those who say that they trust and abide with Him but do not engage in that which pleases Him.

To say 'God is Love' we may need to look at how He loves without wavering, no matter what we have done as mankind to Him. He showed me Adam's sin for what it was - a betrayal of a deep interactive love in a moment of time with total disregard for the relationship. It was a disgusting slap in the face of Him who loved us beyond everything! Adam, in a moment, rejected He who created us, nurtures us and who gave us life! After this revelation, He journeyed me through time to Jesus and Father's need to do whatever it takes (within the bounds of who He is) to redeem man from the cost of his betrayal. Father has always been "HOLY" toward us. (That is: "to be set apart unto"). With Jesus, He opened a way for us to experience redemption and experience being whom

He created us to be. There is no way for me to explain in words the cost to Father, Jesus and Holy Spirit for our redemption. Nor can I truly explain His unwillingness to be other than "Love" to us. *He has paid an enormous price to love us the way we need to be loved*, that He would "save" us from our sin! Father gave us a part of Himself, His son - the second Adam, to redeem us from our betrayal, counting us as "the pearl of great price."

We can experience "being Love" through Jesus, but to do so we will need to lay down some deeply entrenched lies and traditions of man and religion.

We were created in God's image and in His likeness. Jesus' sacrifice restored us to that original position and an even better place through His never-ending covenant. Most people who have given their lives to Jesus know that obedience is a big thing to Father. However, most obey out of fear of disapproval or think that a failure to obey will bring God's wrath or judgment.

They do not understand His true nature. Religious obedience is a works-based obedience to a higher authority and does not result in freedom, instead it produces a relationship like with a boss that you are afraid of because he is capable of sudden anger and destructive tendencies. It produces a fear-based obedience which will never produce what Father created for us. Obedience out of a close, personal, dynamic, naturally supernatural (intimate) relationship with God is based on trust and the "needs of the relationship." **Every relationship, whether with God or man, has requirements** based on the individual needs of each party and how much you treasure the other party in the relationship. I call this "the need of the relationship." People need to know, participate in and experience love; they need to be needed, to truly want to continue in a relationship. That is the "need" of the relationship. Father loves us first, but He is also hungry to be loved! He desires our presence and has made a way for us to be in relationship. He has paid the ultimate price for our attention. Our obedience to live with Him and honor Him and His desires make our love real and not just words to Him.

So, our "obedience" is not based upon "I must." Our obedience is founded on our "need" or desire to know Him. I like being in His presence. So, to cultivate His presence I do things with Him that I know interests Him. My "obedience" is simply a response or reaction to being loved and appreciating Him for His care. Intimacy with God and trusting obedience are the central themes of the Bible, and circle around the "power of choice" which is a must in Love. **If we have no choice, then there is no love!** Throughout the Word we see the results of "choice", good and bad ones. I re-iterate; *my obedience is my choice and the way to show trust and love to Father, Jesus and Holy Spirit.*

This obedience, through my choices, is the result of a true relationship.

It is a response to being loved in a real way! It is the evidence of my trust. To say I was overwhelmed with the experience I had in that hotel room with a fly and at the restaurant with the people there would be an understatement. In that time, I was experiencing a response from Father to my quest to know Him and His heart. It was a beginning as Father also showed me what it is like to "be love" rather than just give love. There was such a sense of faith I felt that seemed so present in me and trustworthiness was seen by the people and the fly. The time was an exhibition of His love and what would happen if we allowed ourselves to be who we were created to be and lived in the confidence of His promises. That experience was in 1983. Today, I am still having revelations from that time.

Three days with a fly changed my perceptions and my identity drastically. It put me on a quest for a deeper intimacy and understanding of Father that continues today. After my experience with God and this fly, I was called home by my employer.

Two weeks later I came back to this same motel with my wife to finish my work in the area. I asked her to come, hoping she might experience what had happened to me because she is my best friend. (*So many things I experience do not seem real until she is a part of them*)! After checking in at about 7 pm, Dana and I went to the restaurant to get some food. When we entered, there was the man who had come to me the second day of my fly experience, with his wife and some others.

He hugged me and told me how he had left the restaurant after talking with me, went home and confessed his sins and shortcomings to his wife. They had both accepted Jesus and were involved in church already. The wife hugged me and cried a bit then thanked me for changing her husband. The next morning at breakfast, the three waitresses all came and hugged me, then all came to our booth when they could and told how their lives had been changed. They had all returned to or received Jesus also! I was confounded by these people's actions, as I had not given them any advice nor told them about Jesus. It was His Perfect Love that had to have changed them. I believe this experience should be the norm of Christ in us, lived out daily. My constant prayer is to experience His presence for others daily!

God's perfect love never fails (1Cor. 13:8**) and casts out fear (**1 Jn.4:18**).** *Furthermore* **we are sent to be perfect love, just like Jesus***! (Jn. 20:21)*

Proverbs 16:7 states that *"When a man's ways please the Lord, He will cause even his enemies to be at peace with him."*

One of the revelations that came at that time was in the form of a question from the Lord. He asked, "What does Beelzebub, (one of satan's names) mean?" The answer: 'Lord of the flies." That in itself was a huge revelation and caused me to have a whole different perspective of Father, my position with Him and how that affects ALL whom I encounter, including satan. ***Our identity and perspective make such a difference in the way we respond to others and how they respond to us.***

1 Cor. 13:13, (NKJV) And now abide faith, hope, and Love, these three but the greatest of these is Love, (God's Love, His naturally supernatural presence that changes what can not be changed and gives what is needed because it is what is needed). His love creates intimacy; a close dynamic, personal, naturally supernatural expression of His interaction with and through us. My definition of the word - Agape', (God's kind of Love), my thoughts about life in Jesus, being "born again", and having the Spirit of God in me and on me have never been the same. My perspective of 1 Cor.13 being "the powerless love chapter" that we revert to when we have

'nothing more powerful to give' changed. My thoughts on 1 Cor.12, and the "power of the Spirit with us and on us", moving through believers being more powerful than Love was destroyed because my definition of "God's Love" changed.

God's Love is always naturally supernatural in expression and changes that which can not be changed without HIS presence because He IS Love!

Paul says at the end of chapter 12, "… and yet I show you a more excellent way." - that does not say a "less powerful way." It says a more excellent one! Love (agape') is Jesus and Father's presence. With them   present how many of the "gifts of the Spirit" are present with you?

Through the years, the experience of those 3 days comes up and I get new revelations or thoughts from the memory of it. I still wonder at that encounter and wait for a full understanding of all that happened. One thing I know and that is that Father definitely has a sense of humor and knows how to mess me up! He knew I was raised around cattle, sheep, horses, feedlots and that flies are everywhere in that lifestyle. They are one of my most UNFAVORITE insects! To use a fly to demonstrate His love and its power was sneaky to say the least.

The testimony of the "fly experience" always brought a lot of laughter and then, each time, revelations to those who have heard it. **This experience and revelation of His Love came as a result of a continual persistent perseverance and working at a relationship for years; a friendship I did not know how to fathom.** *The fly encounter could be an encounter with anyone, a* friend, a foe, the enemy or? The waitresses and people in the restaurant and their response to me, as I embraced God's presence and revelations of the reality of His love abiding in me, show just what is possible if we embrace being known by Him and to know Him. It was Christ in me they saw and trusted. His presence still does the impossible and brings us to life! What if we believed what scripture says about us? His promises and provision are not just written promises, but spoken realities.

Scripture is a written witness of what Father has spoken. It is promises and provision to guide man to be what man was created to be. Jesus is our model of being Love, the example lived out of who created man is. My experience with that fly, and the people, reveals the life we are meant to live as His creation.

What if we abandoned ourselves to His provision, promises and position or identity? I believe we need a fresh perspective and a revelation of our true identity in Jesus and our true nature bought by His Blood sacrifice.

Insignificance/Significance;

I do not know how many times I have been confronted with these following statements from people I have met or taught around the world, "I would love Jesus to use me like He does you. I don't have enough training and do not know enough scriptures to pray like you do, God does not talk to me like He does to you." "I am not adequate or worthy of Him speaking to me". What these people are saying is, "I am not really significant (valuable) to Christ or in church. God has favorites and I am not one of them". Other statements like, "I don't have the faith to pray in public, what if God does not answer my prayer, I might make a mistake and embarrass pastor or disappoint God with my prayers. My life does not measure up, I could never pray like that as I am just not good enough." These statements, and others like them, show us that most of the body of Christ exists in a place of wrong identity and perspective, though many would not tell you that.

Somehow most of the Church has come to the place of living in doubt, fear, and insignificance. Less than 7% of the body of Christ is involved in obedience to the "GO" commands found in the Gospels. Not being perfect (according to our traditional idea of perfect) or holy enough is thought to be a sin which causes most of us to feel insignificant in our minds. Thus, the promises and commands of God are beyond us. We are not worthy of His presence, power and love. We do not feel we are valuable enough for Him to need our prayers or actions of obedience. Our own view of "our" unimportance keeps us from receiving the truth that He is hungry to be a part of our lives, that He needs us. Most do not believe or comprehend they are significant to Him, resulting in many of the people sitting in a self-imposed prison inadvertently created by man's tradition and the hierarchy found in the church. This is somewhat like being in an open empty cave, a self-imposed prison of sorts, just out of the light, without value.

This next vision shows how much we limit ourselves when we think we are insignificant, and not worthy, when in reality God is longing for us to discover and live in our true identity as His sons and daughters. Jn.8:36 (NKJV), "Whom the Son sets free is free indeed!"

The Cave;

This dream came early in my "Christian life" or my life after I surrendered to Jesus' Lordship, and was a foundation for me to continue to go to the lost and hurting… My hope is this; that what I share will trigger you to remember things that the Lord has spoken to you to encourage you to continue, or to help direct you down the path He has for you. You are valuable to God and not insignificant! Many times we don't want to hear, so we will question what we know is God. If we truly hear what Father has said, it will cause us to have to admit something or to change our opinion of ourselves. Most of what I get I would call visions, because they happen when I am awake sitting with my Lord or praying. This one came while I was sleeping on my favorite couch one afternoon, so it should be called a dream. The Lord brought this back to me recently and reminded me that basically we all have the same calling – "seek and save the lost" and "destroy the works of the enemy."

It also talks about how most of the church body feels about themselves as being insignificant. Our Identity, perspective and position affect what we hear and experience.

No one is insignificant or of no value to the Lord…

I found myself in a cave-type cell, with no door on the front, with about a dozen people in it with me. I knew it was a prison, but it was unique. There were many cave cells along the edge of a mountain and the front of all of them was wide open. There were no locks or fences in this place. One of the men in the cave with me was lying on a mat and was sickly and weak, like he was an over-worked and abused slave. There were no marks on his flesh from any beatings, but the perception of abuse was there. Another man was so depressed he was constantly muttering over and over,

"There is no way out of here, there is no escape, I have no future." He was resigned to the fact that this pitiful existence in this open type prison was all there would ever be. In his mind he had a life sentence of meaningless existence.

I wandered this prison area freely and no one touched me, though some of the people in this prison were my friends or people that I had met in a variety of places. I could see the guards at times. They were huddled together watching me to see what I would do. It was like they were waiting for some signal from the warden. They would leer at me and mock me a lot. As I passed people I knew or stopped to talk with someone, all would tell me that it was impossible to escape and that no one had ever made a successful attempt.

It seemed that the sickly, weak fellow and the mental case I had met first were close friends of mine, although I did not know any names in the vision/dream. Whenever anyone told me there was no escape I would reply, "Have faith, we are going to get out of here." I informed these two men that I had first met that I was taking them with me and we would escape.

When I spoke this it caused them great concern. Their reaction to my words showed that they felt hopeless, insignificant and of little value. Everyone there seemed consumed with fear! As I wandered this prison area, I noticed that the guards never touched anyone physically. They would stand over them and torment them with words. Also, their impressive physical presence would intimidate or dominate the prisoners through fear inducing tactics. They constantly told these people that they were worthless, of no value or no good and that they would die in this place. They would accuse them of horrible things and constantly tell them that there was no escape. One of these men worked in a garden tilling the ground that grew nothing. Everything in this place was demeaning and discouraging! There was at least one guard over each man and some had several over them. All of these guards utilized the same tactics; constant verbal attacks and yelling in their captive's face with whatever words it took to demean, defeat and disgrace them.

All jobs there required you to work bent over or be on your knees. The innuendos changed from person to person and were always very personal, yet there was a common theme through them all – "*you are worthless!*"

The same tactic worked differently in each man. Some became depressed, others angry but hopeless, still others lost their physical strength as a result of the onslaught. The common theme among the prisoners seemed to be one of hopelessness and unreasonable fear. As the days went by people were always stopping me, warning me that soon it would be my turn to be tormented. At each of these incidents I would reply with, "Have faith and we will get out of here." Most times they would reply with,

"No one has ever escaped, you don't understand! The warden wants you to try to escape and he will let you go. But in the morning, they always bring you back. Eventually you will give up and surrender to the fact that you cannot escape". I witnessed this same scenario happening almost every evening and night. Someone would attempt to escape and the guards would just watch, mock those leaving and laugh. Then in the morning, the prisoners would come back to camp, being herded by the guards. The warden mocked them and humiliated them before all the other prisoners for their foolish attempt at leaving. It was quite a show and I watched as one after the other eventually gave up their hope and resigned themselves to the fact that they had no value and would never escape. **At *this time, I had a vision in the vision; I felt that people's unwillingness to see the truth and their fear of taking responsibility for their own lives and salvation seemed to be the main blockage or reason for the prisoners living insignificant and imprisoned.***

The accusations of the warden and guards, and the people's own fears, were the only "fence or gate" that kept all those in the caves from freedom.

Every night I would attend to my friend who was failing physically through the torment he received daily. I would give him part of my food and water rations and then wrap him in my blanket to warm him. I would talk to my friend, who was mentally depressed from the constant railing of the guards and encourage him and others at the end of each day as we sat in the caves. I was always telling these people, "Have faith, we will get out of here." It seemed that my answers always started with, "Have faith."

Each time I would say this someone would reply, *"You just don't understand, you just don't know how bad the guards are. Soon it will be your turn and then you will know. There is no escape! You will never leave here!"* I was amazed at this repeated comment as I had such a confidence I would leave and take others with me; yet I had no actual plan whatsoever. It was like I had this knowing that I did not belong there and neither did these men. Somehow, I knew that what was going on was based on illusion and that any and all of these men could leave if someone showed them the way and they would accept it for the truth. I had no fear of the warden or his guards. Each night I would comfort and encourage those in the open cave with me. Each night was the same; someone would be picked out and tormented all night. The yelling never ceased. The voices never relented. One evening, as I was ministering to the needs of those in the cave with me, the warden and several guards came. The warden pointed at me, while his guards ranted and made threatening gestures, and said, "Tomorrow it is your turn". I was not really impressed, so he ranted on as the guards surrounded me attempting to demean or threaten me with their size and presence. I simply smiled as I stared back at the warden, in perfect peace.

I knew it was the time to leave and that I would take my friends with me and leave that night. After supper, I gathered my mentally depressed friend and the man who was physically weak, and we proceeded to walk out of the compound into the darkness. The guards and the warden howled with laughter as they watched us leave and yelled, "There is no escape!" "You will see." As we left, the ones I took with me were so scared they would constantly tell me that we should give up now and just go back. They really believed there was no escape. (The real problem they had was their beliefs or lack thereof. Their identity was that of menial slaves - not valued sons).

I still had no plan, no idea of how to take these people out of the prison. I did not know what was out there in the darkness. It was a thick, dark, forest type area and no one had ever made it out of the darkness into the light that was just visible in the distance. As we were leaving, the guards were gathering to follow us laughing and talking about how they would break me now. As we walked, I realized that the man who was physically weak could not walk all night so we would need to stop and rest eventually. I received an idea at that moment and smiled inside! I knew the way out! After a short distance I hid them both in a thicket and told them to sleep and rest, we would walk on later. They were both so worried and confused yet they were so tired from the torment that they finally laid down and went to sleep. In the darkness I heard the guards come looking for us. I watched as they went past where we were, and I followed them. After a while they stopped, built a fire, and sat down. I crept up and listened to them discuss and laugh about how they would torment us tomorrow.

They would form a line, and when we came, they would turn us back toward camp. I knew that they were thinking of how they would mock and humiliate our stupidity for our attempt to escape all the way back to the caves. The guards even argued and made bets about how many times I would try to escape before I gave up and was broken. They laughed with glee at the thought of my being turned into a slave. I finally tired of listening to their arrogance and went back to my friends that I had hidden. I let them sleep till just before dawn, then got them up and we headed back toward the camp.

Their fear at heading back toward the camp was immense and I had to constantly encourage them that I knew what I was doing. As we walked into the camp, the others thought we had been defeated and wondered where the warden and guards were? They watched as we walked straight through the camp, out the other side and into the forest. Soon we were walking in the light, and we were free. (I felt that some of those in the camp followed us out of curiosity and maybe a bit of hope, but am not sure how many). We had outwitted the warden and had escaped! I had brought my friends with me and we were free! I awoke from this dream as the Lord spoke to me. "Today you have escaped the camp of the enemy, I am always before you and if you continue to follow Me, and look to Me, you will remain free. The enemy will always be behind you waiting. If you look back, you will feel his torment. He will always be waiting to torment and destroy your faith in Me or kill you, if he can. I have called you, as I do all who find me and hear me, to set the captives free!" There were many lessons and Words from the Lord as a result of this dream.

Through the years, I have thought on this dream as it has brought me confidence to "go" into the camp of the enemy many times to snatch someone from his clutches.

One of the lessons learned was that the enemy has only intimidation, fear, and deception to hold us imprisoned, depressed and feeling insignificant; to keep us from "going!" He cannot touch us unless we agree with him or let him. "**Have faith**!" is the cry of our God and savior. The Lord has a plan, *we need to trust and obey because in truth there is no other way out of the enemy's hand*. Father's love has an answer to all of the enemy's insinuations and torments. **His love never fails,** and **He does need us all**!

This dream showed me that I could take some of my friends with me (out of the enemy's hands), no matter their problem. It also showed me that it was my choice to stay or go, I was not bound in the enemy's cave nor were any of those there. I had to choose to stay, to take them with me, or to leave by myself. My confidence was actually an exhibition of my faith. My confession (the words I spoke) brought to existence what was God's will. "Have faith" was simply the expression of my heart that Jesus would make a way. My lack of fear was infuriating to the enemy. He is still behind me and at times I have looked back and felt his torment. I always get up and walk on, looking to Jesus, the author and finisher of my faith! The Lord goes before me… I am free! As long as I keep my eyes on Him I have no fear! This vision has brought me to a more intimate place with Father and Jesus as I ponder the strength of His Spirit to protect me and guide me, to lead me as He promised in Romans 8:14-17.

Fear of what men think and our hidden insecurities (pride) will lead us to live in a prison without bars. The good news - you don't have to stay there! <u>You are not insignificant, nor does your fear of not being good enough come from Father!</u>

The reality of our position in our mind and heart affects how and what we hear from those we interact with, including God. Our impact on those we interact with is affected by; how we see ourselves in Christ, how we see others and how we think they see us. **The position we see ourselves in** with God affects how we interact with those in our world. It also **affects our conversations with Him.** God has delivered some incredible statements of His love for us and the position we inhabit in His plan. He has centered His attention on us.

We are the "pearl of great price" to Him. I know that we say we are "sons" (or daughters) of God. (1Jn. 3:2-4, Gal.3:26-4:7). Yet for the most part when we say it, we say it to show others how privileged we are. There seems to be almost haughtiness to our speaking, "We are sons of God!" "Bless God, WE have arrived!" We seem to feel that we "deserve" to be lifted up and exalted by those around us. We expect privileges to be thrown our way. It's like we feel that most people should give us breaks, show us favor and give things to us just because we are the children of God. In reality, if you look at all of the Scriptures that speak to us about being sons of God, you might find that there is a responsibility and humility to the position. How can we say that we are sons of God and not show responsibility toward God and His purpose? In John 20:21 the Lord tells us that we are sent just like He was sent. If I look at that scripture correctly, I believe that it is telling me that I have a responsibility to honor God and to serve Him in righteousness and integrity, as a son, to my death. Honoring God through trusting obedience must be seen by the way we live all of the time. The Scriptures found in 1 John 3: 2-4, Galatians 3:26-4:7 and 2 Peter 1:2-4 all show that we are in a favored position with God. But they also should speak to us about having a responsibility to reveal His kingdom and kingship to the world. Our living should show that He is a good King who loves people and hates evil. We must be responsible children bringing others to trust in His Name.

Read John.10:3-5,16,27; 14:26;15:26;16:8-13, Romans 8:14-17. These and other NT scriptures tell us we should all hear and know God's voice personally and thus, know Him. That is The Truth! Hearing God and knowing Him, (that is having a close, personal, dynamic, intimate communion with Him) is a rudimentary, foundational requirement of Christianity. You cannot even come to God unless you hear Holy Spirit! (Jn.16:8-13). The Scriptures that I've just stated that you should know, should bring us to the place of looking at our "significance", not our "insignificance." In many traditional church gatherings, leaders actions and that which happens as a result, show the church body their significance and the "lay" people's insignificance.

Most believers are taught **inadvertently**, through leaders' actions, that they occupy the position of insignificance. I do not believe this is intentional. It is what is taught to the leaders in our Christian colleges.

The results of doing "church" with a clergy-laity foundation that is taught to our leaders, where clergy hear God and dictate what is God and what is not God, causes many in the Body of Christ to feel insignificant in church. This is so wrong and against what Jesus models for us. Whatever we do to those we think are "the least", we do to Jesus!

I can be quite frustrated at the clergy/laity system that leave many in the Body feeling insignificant and of little value. Jesus says in Matthew 20:25-28 that leaders are to be the least, **serving ALL** others. Paul says in Ephesians 4:11-15 that they are given *as servants* to the body to **lift-up** (edify) and **give the body tools,** (equip the Body) so that the BODY can do the *work of ministry*. The Body was not given to them. Peter says in 1Peter 5:1-5 for leaders to serve NOT as lords over people but by being *examples* to the flock. *The body of Christ has NOT been given to the leaders for their agenda. Leaders are given to the body to serve and lift up others "till all come to the unity of faith and the fullness of the Christ."*

The CHURCH BODY is to do the *ministry! The fact that in a traditional church setting it is hard to do our gatherings differently lends to leaders controlling meetings and only a few doing most of the ministry. It is a difficult pattern to change when it has been handed down for a long time as the pattern we should live. The clergy/laity system has become the "Norm." Leaders are doing what they know, but we need to go back to scripture and help all find significance in Christ.* Church traditions tend to re-enforce the idea of most Christ followers being unimportant by default or a lack of understanding.

What we do speaks to those around us. The actions and leadership style found in many traditional church settings inadvertently let the people sitting in the pews know they do not hear as well as those leading. Those who are deemed significant are the ones up front leading. Their actions and prayers matter and for the most part the rest of the body becomes "un-involved", except to serve in the church building and to give to the leader's vision and needs. By sitting in the "congregation" week after week, listening to those who are always in front, most feel that their obedience to Christ and relationship with Christ is not nearly as "intimate" or as important as those who dictate what scripture is saying. <u>Each person in the Body of Christ should KNOW Him and KNOW they are needed by Him and **significant** in the Body!</u> "Each joint of two members brings something to the body" Eph. 4:13-17 – two or three believers coming together supplies for a need of the body and IS Church. Each person and union in the body is important to GOD. By default or design, your ancestor leaders have twisted scriptures to create a "clergy/laity" setting in Christ's body. Thus, we have created first and second-class citizens of the kingdom. Rather than go back to scripture and admit that we are in the wrong according to scripture, we continue to "BEND" God's Word to justify our practices. _We all have the potential to twist the scriptures or leave some of them out when they come against our practices or comfort._ Our practices show that there is a hierarchy in the body in-spite of God's dictated Word that states "the greatest of these SHALL be the servant of all" – not a lord over! The enemy is the accuser of the brethren! Our 'need' for comfort, acceptance by our friends in the world, and for life to be non-confrontational, thus compatible with the world's standard, has brought us to the place we live today. Traditions and acceptance in the world seem more powerful than The Word of God in much of our modern Christianity. (I am at fault as much as anyone else). It is time for repentance and a change.

Intimacy with God;

Sitting in the Throne of Grace with Jesus;

As I was writing this next section on Intimacy with God, I hope what I have written does justice to the body of Christ finding a close, personal, dynamic, intimate fellowship with My Father!

One day I was sitting in my chair meditating on Jesus, not having anything to pray for coming to mind, but just wanting to be in His presence. I told Him that I would simply like to come for a visit, sit and watch Him in the Throne of Grace. The next moment, I found myself in what I can only describe as a hall type area. I could see Jesus sitting next to His throne on some steps leading up to it. The hall had marble floors and scattered around the interior were short pillars. On these pillars were platters and, on the platters, there was a cup and some bread. (I knew this was His body and blood elements). I was standing in the shadows by one of the walls where there seemed to be some sort of walking area along the edge of the hall. Jesus looked at me smiling at my presence. Somehow, I was able to communicate that I had just come to watch and needed nothing.

As I looked at Him I became aware that someone had entered the hall and was being guided by one of the other beings in the room to one of the short pillars with the Lord's supper on them. As I watched, a person who had entered the room was offered the Lord's supper and after they received it they would turn and leave the room. I would watch Jesus and His expression as this would happen and I was quite moved to see His reaction. Sometimes He would have tears in His eyes, sometimes He would laugh, and His laughter would include a deep joy showing in His eyes. He was never expressionless! Leaning against the wall I was so amazed and content being there. As I continued to watch, a young lady with two small children came into the hall. I turned to watch Jesus and to see what He would do, only to find Him looking at me. I knew He was telling me to go and deliver the bread and wine to her. As I looked into His eyes I let Him know that I had just come to watch and He should have someone else do this. I did not feel worthy or maybe adequate would be a better word for what I conveyed to Him. I saw tears starting to form in Jesus' eyes and realized that they were because of my words. Instantly I replied, "Ok, I will go". This conversation was not so much "spoken" as it was just happening some way beyond my understanding. I proceeded to take the elements to this lady and her two children. When I presented the platter to her she began to cry and you could watch His peace settle over her. I glanced at Jesus and found His eyes brimming with tears of Joy.

After completing His desire, I went back to my position along the wall, watching Him and the proceedings in the Throne Room of Grace. Shortly after this, I saw another person enter the hall and felt Jesus' eyes on me once again.

I turned, and sure enough, He was looking at me and beckoning me to go to this man. I once more started to decline His invitation. There had to be someone more worthy than I. In an instant, the tears were starting to run down Jesus' cheeks. I was so overcome by this display of anguish that I immediately conveyed to Him that I would go, asking Him to please stop crying, With tears I responded, "I am sorry, I will go!" His eyes showed instant joy as I went, and He seemed so happy. When I finished this time and sat the platter back on the short column, Jesus beckoned me to come and sit with Him on the steps by His throne. As I ascended the steps and sat next to Him, He put His arm around me, pulled me close and spoke, (not audible, but it still was His voice), "This is the best place to view what is going on in this place!" As I sat next to Him with His arm around me and His words in my ear, I was overcome by such joy and peace. _This is where I belonged… next to Him!_ As we sat there watching all the events taking place in "The Throne of Grace" hall, every once in a while, He would squeeze my shoulder or lean into me to get my attention, to look **with** Him at something special going on. As we would watch together, He would then turn and look into my eyes, many times with tears of Joy, and we would share something profound beyond words – a moment of oneness filled with emotion and joy! I am not sure how long in real time I was there. I did end up back in my chair in our house and instantly I received a revelation of our time together in the Throne Room.

The Throne of Grace is a place in the spirit where people's prayers from earth come into the presence of Jesus. It is where Jesus then calls on someone on earth to go to the person with a need, bring Christ's presence and provision to them to see them changed by His love given through us.

When He nudges us or moves us spiritually for someone and then we say we are not worthy or are insignificant, we break Jesus' heart! He needs us! It hurts Him when we believe the enemy's lies and say His sacrifice is not enough, that we are not enough in Him.

 He gave all, that we may **ALL** be "like Him." Jn.20:21-23

Through the years of walking with Jesus and surrendering to His will and direction I have been a part of many miracles and wonders. I have seen a leg grow to full length on a girl in India who was a polio victim and had a leg about 6" long before we prayed. I have seen a cancerous tumor fall off a lady in Indonesia. I have seen demons flee, and people set free with simply a touch and no words (scripture says we will lay hands on people, and they will recover). While preaching in a small town in NV, a whole room of people were knocked out of their chairs and laid out in the Lord with the sweep of my arm while I was talking about Jesus not being divided, (1 Cor. 1:1-18). I have seen cattle healed by anointing them with oil. I have witnessed un-broke horses tamed without putting a halter or bridle on them with Jesus presence, and I have seen rain fall on a rectangular farm acreage through prayer and declarations the Lord told me to make while working as an electrician for an irrigation company in Idaho.

Crops have been changed in several countries through prayer and anointing the land with oil. As I have walked with Jesus through the years, I have also seen families restored and made whole from anger, bitterness, fear, abuse, etc., just by His presence. Several times I have sat with Jesus and Father in Heaven as they asked me questions or gave me revelations on subjects I was inquiring about.

I realize I am not special, and that what I have experienced can be had by anyone willing to engage and **know** Jesus and Father. I have been so privileged and humbled at all that the Lord has done in my life. I was healed of a broken neck at 17 and of severe burns at 32. At work, during these years of living with Jesus, I have many times been saved from severe injury by the Lord. Yet, **In reality,** *those miracles, though they revealed God's love and power in amazing ways to people I have encountered while sharing His Truth and Grace, are not enough to reveal all that intimacy with Father and Jesus is about.*

My Lady Dana is the one Jesus used the most. She has taught me about commitment, intimacy and what real love is about! She has shown me what it is to persevere in love. She never gives up on me, always is looking at ways to get me to be better at who I am and no matter what I have done, she has stood as a true helpmate in Jesus. Dana never lets me get away with sayings like. "I don't know." She has caused me to face the truth and grow. It is her confidence in me that gives me the strength to go beyond what I think I can do and be more than I am capable of. When we have "enthusiastic conversations," she will usually be the one who finds Jesus in the midst of it and shows His attitude quicker than me. She is quite prophetic and when I am traveling her calls to me, or texts usually will be right on point. What we talk about on the phone while I am overseas ends up being included or leading me in what is happening where I am, and with what I share. <u>When we agree on anything it is done</u>, because she agrees with her heart not just in her head, and she has taught me to do the same. As God began this "intimacy training" with me so long ago

He told me that He would teach me how to love Him by showing me how to love my wife *the way she needs to be loved, not the way I wanted to.* (*I am sure that even after all these years I still have actions and words that are not showing my Love to*

either Dana or Father and Jesus in a way that I would really like to. But this I do, I press on!)

To begin to understand intimacy with God you must figure out that it is not about what you **get** out of the relationship, it is what you **give out of the need of** the relationship! If God's love for man is sustained out of what He gets back from man, His love is definitely not working well. Why would He continue? God loves us because He IS Love. **God's kind of Intimacy, that grows and is without end, is a dedicated choice without withdrawal privileges and without conditions of response imposed on those that you choose to share this Love with.** Father's naturally supernatural love is about the needs of others, yet always abides in the truth and is founded in integrity, accountability and righteousness. "It takes honor, obedience and sacrifice…" (one of Lady Dana's statements).

I still have no idea of how to truly illustrate my "intimacy" with God and its effect on others, or how to define in practical terms the length, width, depth, and height of God's Love.

When we were moving from the Roseburg, Oregon, area to our present location north of Spokane, Washington, a group of our friends gathered with us for a meal prior to our departure. This story, from that gathering, illustrates how I purpose to be instant in season and out of season to hear and trust the Spirit in me,

to guide my conversations in a way that will affect those I am around no matter what I am doing. Two of the men, at this going away gathering, had been friends of mine for 8-10 years. We visited each other occasionally, ate some meals together, and we had attended Christian gatherings and prayer meetings together. They had also attended a few trainings on intimacy/discipleship, etc. that Dana and I had put on through the years. One of the men told me every year that He would take me salmon fishing in his boat. He was known as a good salmon fisherman, and I really enjoy fishing. So each year I would look forward to a trip with him. Not a single trip ever happened. The other guy would tell me that he was going to take me golfing. Again, each year I would hear this and look forward to it. It also never happened in all the time I was around him. At this gathering, I cornered the two of them and asked them both this question; "Why is it that both of you would tell me that you were going to call me and take me fishing or golfing, but in all the years we have been friends it never happened? I would remind you both occasionally but could never get either to set a date."

They looked at each other then one of them said, "Since you are leaving, I guess I can tell you. I just could not spend 5 hours with you fishing because I knew you would 'read' my mail (know about his life) and I did not want to change or have you expose to me my hidden sins"! "The other guy just laughed and agreed with one word, "Exactly!" We all had a good laugh and many others agreed with them that being around me was dangerous as Father was always telling me something about someone.

*They were right. If I spend that many hours with someone, Father is probably going to show me things about them that I cannot know outside of it being Holy Spirit revelations - and we **will** talk about them!* It is the truth that sets people free and if I really love them then I must be truthful and be willing to be vulnerable to HS for them. This story is funny in a way, but if you are an intimate friend with someone, they share things with you about other people in their lives. Why would it be different with Father? We are friends with Him and He is always about people and their freedom. I am a man given to dreams, visions and conversations with Father. I know things about people as well as things to come because <u>I am a friend of God's</u>! I am not a special person, just vulnerable to my best friend, I enjoy **HIS** company. I know that God's promises are true as I have tried Him and know Him. I do not follow Jesus because of His promises but because He is God. He can be a bit overwhelming at times and He is not tame, but He is all about people! Abandoning and surrendering my life to Him is the only way to live! **Sometimes His voice just is and He can say more in a nano-second that I can speak in a month.**

Our Identity;

Identity determines our perspective and actual position in Jesus.

If you abide in me and my words abide in you, THEN you will ask... His Words are not just those found in the Bible we read. Scripture is a testimony of Him and a guide to Him, (Jn.5:39). There is much more He has to say than what is found in 'The Word!" It is a foundation and guide, but the relationship the Bible reveals in its pages needs the reality of a true close friendship connection, a family relationship and communion.

Two words, **Trust** and **Entrust,** seem to be defining words in my close, personal, dynamic, (intimate) relationship with Father. These words are not really spoken between us as much as understood, felt or implied by our actions in the relationship.

"Trust" is two-edged as is "entrust." Both are present in a close intimate relationship. On my part, trust is displayed by my willingness to obey Father's directions and commands (His precepts). By putting my life and future in Father's Hands;

thus, *I entrust myself to Father's care and protection.* On Father's part, He entrusts me with other's care and anticipates my obedience to do His commands; thus, fulfilling His desire to show His naturally supernatural Love to others through me. (*He entrusts me with His kingdom and the future of others*).

The future is in the hands of "our" relationship or interactions. Our commitment to one another and our relationship with each other will be the determining factor that develops God's Kingdom and fulfills His purpose in my world and those around me. The foundation of all we do has to be started with "What is God's purpose or goal?" On any trip you take there has to be a beginning point and a destination in place to begin the trip and to keep you on the right road or path as you GO. <u>Without a purpose there is no reference point or focus</u>, thus we end up wandering instead of going somewhere. In Christianity this is the same. What is our destination or focus to be? We all begin with surrender and repentance, but for what purpose? What is Christ's purpose and Father's goal?

At the age of thirty I made Jesus LORD, not just Savior of my life. This transfer of ownership caused quite a stir in my family as it was a 180-degree turn from my previous living, which was all about "ME". I knew Jesus as Savior from the age of 17 and we had been friends from the age of 11, but I had not known Him as LORD.

Because of this decision, I began to devour the Word of God daily. We went to "church" where I learned to pray as I watched others pray and speak to God. I became a zealous, religious being. My mind was pulling me to "know" how to be a "good Christian", **but my heart** was hungry for Jesus and His presence - to **know** Him. Every time I went to a meeting, I was taking notes and making notations in the empty pages in my Bible. I marked up the whole thing, even the inside pages, with interpretations of scripture I was being taught. It was awesome! But, because of the hunger in my heart to know more about Jesus, I was a sore spot on many leaders' backside, as I was always asking questions that were outside the "being submissive" place I was expected to live in as a "new Christian." I questioned authority structures and the way meetings were run. Yet, even in this questioning, hungry time I was swallowing much that I was taught about scripture, my position in the body and my purpose that they were teaching. We started in a Free Methodist Church and then after a period of time there we were told my "gift mix" was needed elsewhere. So, we migrated to a Faith Church, to a charismatic fellowship, then to a Baptist congregation, an Assembly of God and even a Salvation Army post. I was hungry and learned a lot from each personal and church experience, Bad and good. All of our experiences taught me something about Christianity and Christ, as I received all of them from "The Hand of the Lord." Much of my time at home was spent in study and reading. I would pray for hours and cry to God for more understanding and a greater revelation of who He is. I was preaching at cowboy meetings, at retreats, churches, and in parks. We were seeing signs and wonders happen.

There were healings and prophetic words that came to pass, people got delivered from their past and demonic influences. A bunch of "failures" showed up also - places where I missed God and did not do as He spoke. We learned as much through them as we did with the successes, as they drove us to God and His scripture to find answers as to why. It was an amazing time! I was hungry for something that I could not find anywhere I went. Though I had had my experience with the fly and other supernatural events, I did not know what I was looking for. I knew some truth, had some revelations and some interesting spiritual experiences with Father, but the relationship I was still hungering for was still out there for me to discover - the one I wanted that would change my life and those around me forever. Though I did a lot of study on "God's Love," I still was not receiving what I was looking for. **All of my revelations ended up being about "doing" ministry and not about 'living" life with Jesus.** Though I had grown and learned some vital concepts about Christ and His Word, after about 4-5 years of ministry and years of "traditional church life," I was still in a place of frustration and hunger. At one point, He instructed me to buy a new bible and start fresh with no markings to guide me, no references to other passages, and no notes. He had me start in the book of John and told me to listen as I read and to read what it said. It was an amazing time, and I cried a lot as I read, because I realized that like many others, <u>I had been taught to read the Bible through what others said it meant</u>. Much of what I was taught was _**NOT**_ what the Bible actually said. _The teachers and leaders I had had were not trying to deceive anyone;_ they were teaching what they had been taught the Word said.

A foundational teaching in Christianity is "Receive Jesus so you get to go to heaven and not go to hell." I was taught the goal of salvation was heaven, where we will sit around the throne and praise God for eternity. In studying the concept of eternal life, I came across John 17:3, and my understanding of eternal life changed.

Eternal life is not about heaven or hell for that matter, Both are by-products. It is about relationship. John 17:3 says that "eternal life" is to **KNOW** the Father and His Son, Jesus. This revelation caused me to begin to study and cross-reference the word "**know.**" By doing that, I found some interesting scriptures about relationship. During that same time frame while I was doing a ministry somewhere and as I was studying, Holy Spirit took me to Matthew 7:21-23 and Luke 13:22-27.

Mt.7:21-23: (NKJV)

"Not everyone who says to Me, 'Lord, Lord,' shall enter the kingdom of heaven, but he who does the will of My Father in heaven. 22 Many will say to Me in that day, 'Lord, Lord, have we not prophesied in Your name, cast out demons in Your name, and done many wonders in Your name?' 23 And then I will declare to them, **I never knew you; depart from Me,** you who practice lawlessness!' (Emphasis mine)

Lu.13:22-27 (NKJV)

22 And He went through the cities and villages, teaching, and journeying toward Jerusalem. 23 Then one said to Him, "Lord, are there few who are saved?" And He said to them, 24 "Strive to enter through the narrow gate, for many, I say to you, will seek to enter and will not be able. 25 When once the Master of the house has risen up and shut the door, and you begin to stand outside and knock at the door, saying, 'Lord, Lord, open for us,' and He will answer and say to you, 'I do not know you, where you are from,' 26 then you will begin to say, 'We ate and drank in Your presence, and You taught in our streets.'

27 **But He will say, 'I tell you I do not know you, where you are from. Depart from Me, all you workers of iniquity.' (Emphasis mine).**

While reading these passages He told me, "Neil, you do not know me and I do not know you!" THAT shook me and caused me to realize that all my "doing" was not of much value without "knowing" and being "known" first. I was casting out demons, teaching, preaching, eating in His presence. In these scriptures from Matthew and Luke, He told me I was a worker of iniquity! We had NO intimacy! I found, through these scriptures and a few others, that intimacy WITH Jesus should be preemptive to my "doing" anything for Jesus that would matter. Traditional teaching and doctrines had forgotten a very important detail - **to know and be known by God is the foundation and goal of Christ**. Our relationship with Jesus and Father through Holy Spirit makes a big difference in the outcome of our obedience as our motivation for obeying is changed. Obedience becomes compulsive because it is about Honor and Love. When I got this revelation, I was broken, confused and mad all at once. Eternal life is to **know** (have a close, intimate, dynamic, personal relationship and fellowship with God the Father, Jesus His Son, and Holy Spirit. It is similar to the relationship Adam had with Father in the garden in the beginning, only better!

Salvation is not about getting to heaven or out of hell — those are byproducts of "knowing or not knowing God" in a real way! This word "know" changes everything, especially our focus. This brings a reality to much of what Jesus taught, modeled and revealed in His living on earth as a man. If intimacy with man is the goal of God's salvation (eternal life), then God's creation of man makes sense.

We are made for fellowship with God, to be a companion or friend in a **real** relationship with our creator. We, mankind, are to be like God (not God but <u>like</u> God). Then God can have fellowship with someone who understands Him. Wow, what a concept—to be a companion of God's, a part of the family and not in a religious way. (In Genesis it says we are created in His likeness and in His image).

The concept of hearing the voice of God daily and responding to Him in a real relationship is foreign, or at the least it is limited, to most who call themselves Christian. For the most part, Christians leave hearing God's voice to leaders or elders. They live in a place with feelings of insignificance or irrelevance. They have the opinion that you must be someone of importance to have God talk to you and give you insight into the spiritual realm. <u>Tradition</u> has "bent" the truth of intimacy to fit the agenda or desire of those in the positions of authority. **Traditional Church doctrine predominately teaches us that a person must be very learned and have a deep understanding of scripture to be able to have a "real" relationship with God. Without a long walk with God, doing lots of bible studies, and being in church for a LONG time, a person cannot truly hear the voice of Father or Jesus.**

THAT IS NOT WHAT THE WORD TELLS US!

Intimacy with God is the goal of salvation for all who come to Jesus. <u>ALL are to hear, be known and to know Jesus and His fellowship.</u> At work, and in all of life, God wants to be a part of us and direct us. He needs ALL who follow Christ to "know" Him so He can be made known in all the world and to all the world.

Eternal Life;

Jn 17:3 (NKJV) - "And this is eternal life, that they may know You, the only true God, and Jesus Christ whom You have sent."

Our relationship with Father is shallow because our conversation is shallow. We are still about, "What can we get from Him for us?" We are like toddlers who think that everything is about our needs, our wants and us. **The conversation we have with God reveals the relationship,** never doubt that.

If all we talk of is, "my" needs or wants, the "you promised to give me the desires of my heart" stuff, then where will the conversation go from there?

*What about the desires of **God's heart**? What does He want to talk about or tell us? If it is about us, that is God my Father, Jesus and myself, why is the conversation only about me? Is He not important also?*

The content of our communion tells us how deep our commitment to the marriage or relationship. (God compares our relationship to Him like a marriage relationship or as a Father and His Child in a family relationship).

It does not speak well of the relationship when the conversation is always, "You promised to give me the desires of my heart" or "God you must keep Your promises" or whatever else we say to make the responsibility of the relationship **all** His. An intimate relationship with those thoughts on your mind most of the time will be a most miserable arrangement. I do not hear a lot of prayers that say, "How may I fulfill the desire of your heart today Father"? We do not look at anything that brings "OUR" responsibility to His need in the relationship into focus. What kind of intimacy is that? Shallow at best! We need to tell people the truth; **Jesus did not come to get you to heaven. He came to restore a right relationship between man and God that had been broken.** *__That relationship is eternal life__*. As I have said, *getting to Heaven is simply a by-product of this relationship, as is escaping hell. We have "**BENT**" God's love letter of relationship into a religious proclamation about a relationship that gets us to heaven yet leaves our living without much meaning, purpose or power.*

Our love can be measured, our intimacy can be seen, and our commitment can be weighed. _Our obedience to the relationship shows in our living and the conversations that come out of our heart and mouth._

Are we taking care of the need of the relationship with God or is Father still lonely, looking for fellowship inspite of our salvation? Paul's prayer has been my prayer for a lot of years now and I continue to pray:

Ephesians 3:14-19 (NKJV,)

14 For this reason I bow my knees to the Father of our Lord Jesus Christ, 15 from whom the whole family in heaven and earth is named, 16 that He would grant you, according to the riches of His glory, to be strengthened with might through His Spirit in the inner man, 17 that Christ may dwell in your hearts through faith; that you, being rooted and grounded in love, 18 may be able to comprehend with all the saints what is the width and length and depth and height— 19 to know the love of Christ which passes knowledge; that you may be filled with all the fullness of God.

My wife Dana and I have built our lives around these concepts that are found throughout the New Testament. We are always looking to these words for direction and to check and see where we are spiritually. It is a continual checkup for us. Our goal is to wake up in the likeness of Jesus, living to fulfill Father's desires, whatever the cost, whatever it takes. Paul's prayer for us is our prayer for others; that all may be filled with all the fullness of God!   (One of my favorite verses of all time is:

Psalms. 17:15 (NKJV), "As for me, I will see Your face in righteousness; I shall be satisfied when I awake in Your likeness!

More Jesus, More;

When I started this walk I was a word-eating machine. By that I mean that I had bibles everywhere and there was not many moments when I wasn't working or driving that I was not devouring one. I had bibles and pocket New Testaments, (5 or 6 at least) in a variety of convenient places. Bibles were in every car and room of the house and one was always in my back pocket. I would spend several hours a day studying the bible, reading the Word and I never tired of it or got bored. Studying equated looking up verses that have the same subject matter and putting all of them together so I would get a fullness that created a chain through the scriptures, and I could find a revelation and understanding of whatever subject I was looking up. It was so amazing, this book kept me excited every time I opened it. I eventually had drawers full of my studies. In the midst of that I was always praying for more!

"More Jesus, I want more. I want to wake up in your likeness, whatever the cost!" Even as I immersed myself in the Word, I never seemed to have the "boldness or power" exhibited in the New Testament. I was devouring the Word so why was I not seeing the things I was reading happening in my life? Others I heard about or read about would see miracles, but none were happening where I was living. I concluded that <u>reading was not enough</u>. I knew there had to be something I was missing even with all my studies. Thus, the continued prayer of, "More Jesus!" I would go out into the fields after reading and studying for a while and shout, "Here am I, send me! Touch my lips with the altar's coal, mold me, make me, Father I MUST HAVE MORE!"

My main problem was that I had no idea of what "more" would look like. I had been taught in several fellowships that the "baptism of the Spirit and speaking in tongues." (not the ministry gift of tongues, but the "speaking in tongues" that is part of the baptism in the Spirit) was not relevant for 'our times' and had passed away. I was taught that this "power to be a witness stuff" was no longer necessary or a part of the Christian walk. Good meaning folks and leaders had taught me that we, (The Church), had the Bible now and did not need "that stuff." The Acts 1:4-8 dispensation was past. **THUS,** when I was praying for all that God had and "more." Father was a bit restricted by my tradition taught beliefs. I had limited how He could give me more by not accepting His precepts and provision of more – The Holy Spirit upon, the baptism of the Spirit, being filled with the Spirit (having Him in me and on me).

I had been taught that the "baptism of the Spirit and speaking in tongues" that was to empower us to be a witness was now a deception of the devil and was no longer given by Father. I was persistent though, and never quit asking for more. I needed the boldness I saw in the people of the New Testament (NT). I knew the miraculous was missing in me.

I had an anointing to preach and teach, but though that was exciting, it was not living like Jesus. I was always praying scripture I had read that showed I should be more. (Jn. 14:12,26;15:26; 16:13; 20:21; Acts 1:4-8, 2:4, 4:23-31 and a few others). I would argue with Father about why I didn't have the power and boldness I needed. I prayed, "If you are not a respecter of persons like the Word says, then I want ALL that Paul, Peter and John had! <u>You must give me ALL</u>"! It ended up that Father had to trick me to get me, "The More." I went to work one day and whenever I would get in my vehicle to move or go to another area to do work, I would hear on the radio, "tonight at Boise Junior High." That was it! I would hear no more than that phrase. In my heart I was so convicted that I had to go to this meeting or whatever was happening "Tonight at Boise Junior High". I did not know what it was, who it was about, when it started. I knew nothing but the fact that I Had to be there!!! I rushed home from work, told Dana I had to go to this meeting in Boise and had to leave as soon as I could. I am not sure I sat down for supper. I was so convicted to be at the meeting or event I knew nothing about. I arrived at Boise Junior High at about 6 pm and sat in my car wondering why I was there.

Soon an older couple showed up, parked in front of me and started to unload some boxes to take into the school. Not having anything to do, I offered to carry the boxes for them into the school. There was a table in the hall by the auditorium that we set the boxes on. The couple asked me to watch over the boxes for them until a lady came to take care of them. They wanted to go get a cup of coffee then would be back.

The meeting? – It was about the "Baptism of the Spirit!"

I was so excited because I thought that Father had brought me to see how the enemy worked; to see his deceptions! I sat about 10 rows behind the last one that others sat in. I was going to watch this, how cool!

The teachers were Charles and Francis Hunter whom I had never heard of before. In the "80s" they were a couple who travelled all over the world sharing on the "Baptism of the Spirit" and resulting signs. As Charles began to share scriptures about Holy Spirit (HS), the scripture references he shared were ones I had been praying in my pursuit of "more!" It was intriguing to say the least! As he was sharing, every once in a while, he would point to me, (remember I am 10 rows higher than anyone else in the crowd) and ask me if I could agree with what he was quoting or saying. It was easy to know he was pointing at me as the audience would turn and wait for my response. I was getting a bit uncomfortable with this happening by the time he ended his scripture quotations and asked if anyone in the audience wanted "more." He gave an altar call with, "If you want more power and boldness in Jesus come down here." (Hmmm, that was my prayer for months before this event.) He asked again while pointing at me.

To this day I am sure that someone I could not see grabbed me and pushed me into the aisle and down the steps to the front of the auditorium. Still confused by being thrown down the steps, so to speak, by someone that I could not find behind me, I was not willing to join the crowd so was standing back from those eagerly pressing forward. Once more Charles Hunter began to speak to me and ask me questions. It was weird, why me, why not ask someone else these questions? "Could you pray for all here to get 'more'?

 Can you pray for all Jesus has to be given to all here tonight? Would you pray to receive everything HS has to give?" I nodded as all eyes were on me. Then he said, "Alright then do it, and all of you lift your hands up and surrender to God as this young man prays." Well, I prayed and then found myself speaking in tongues. Gibberish, crazy strange sounds were coming out of my mouth as I opened it to speak. English was not to be found by me at that moment. I rushed from that place mad at God, as I felt He had deceived me, and the devil had given me "tongues!" All the way home I was shouting at God, mad and hurt that He would do this to me! When I arrived home, I stormed into the house with these words, "Father, You will show me that what happened to me is of YOU and scriptural or You and I are done! I will not serve a God who would deceive me and let me receive of the enemy!" I stomped into my study, closed the door and opening my study Bible said, "Ok, show me the scriptures and that what I have experienced is You!" I was up all night as scripture references would come to mind and as I would read them, I would be led to another and another. By the end of the night I realized that what I had been taught by some well-meaning leaders was not the truth!

The baptism of the Spirit was and is of God and in fact Jesus had told His disciples to not try to be a witness without this promise from Father upon them. (Lu. 24:29; Acts 1:4-8). **As much as Jesus' blood made salvation available to all without distinction, the baptism of Holy Spirit makes receiving power and walking like Jesus in this age equally available for all, regardless of**

education or ethnicity. Wow, my living changed as much as a result of that night as my life changed when I surrendered to Jesus. I have not looked back from that experience as I found that God was true to His Word and the Word is true, Jn.14:26, 15:26, and 16:13 are a reality for everyone!

Since that time, miracles, signs and wonders follow us! So many healings and deliverances by Jesus have happened as we fellowship together with others in Christ. Around the world we have seen thousands receive the Baptism of the Spirit resulting in them seeing healings and deliverances. They also have a fresh revelation and understanding of God's scripture through Holy Spirit coming upon them, anointing them just like He did at the beginning of The Church!

I went from Baptist to "Babti-costal" that night; a man of the Word with an Acts 2 experience to live The Word out!

One thing you should know; you don't wake up one day and have all these profound revelations of who God is and who you are to Him. They come in the process of living. They are the product of persistence, sweat and tears. It requires a deep passion and years of consistent yearning and crying out for His heart, and vision for more. This is something that is glossed over when you read a lot of Christian books. People don't talk of the COST that goes into becoming who they are in God. Another thought: Many times, when you ask God for more, you don't have any idea or know what you are asking for, ie: he gave me the baptism of the Spirit and I began speaking in tongues. That was not what I thought I was asking! I just knew I needed "more." I have found through the years what He wants to teach or give me often seems the opposite of what I was expecting or thought I was asking for in our conversations. You can find a paper on our website called "Holy Spirit Upon." I wrote this paper as a result of my experiences that night with God in my study that includes all the scriptures He gave me. It is pretty much written in the order He gave them to me that night with a few definitions and explanations of what was revealed as I read them.

(Some thoughts have been added through the years but mostly it is still what He gave me that night). **As a result of the experience I have just described to you, much of my "Christianity" has changed.** My focus in the Word changed. A new foundation was laid by the Spirit of God. Instead of looking for methodologies and church doctrine, I began to focus on relationship/fellowship with the Lord.

John 5:39 (NKJV) You search the Scriptures, for in them you think you have eternal life; and these are they which testify of Me.

As I began to read and study with a different purpose, I found a lot of things I had learned or come to believe were not actually scriptural, though they were founded in scripture.

Traditions;

There are many beliefs and customs we, "The Church", have picked up through the years and generations. These habits or teachings become what we call, "Traditions". Jesus paid a high price for our sins and these traditions can become very restrictive to the ongoing revelation of the relationship that is to exist between Christ and His body. These traditions, many times, become stronger in us than The Truth.

Tradition: _the handed down beliefs, customs, information etc. from generation to generation. A long-established way of thinking or acting. A continued pattern of culture beliefs and or practices._

(In life it is easy to tell what we believe because we talk about it; BUT what we value we move from just talking about into the realm of DOING!)

_W_**e live what we value!**

Traditions are established to protect what we have learned or received. But many times, these traditions establish, "take the place of", or restrain us from doing what we have discovered in His Word that should change our relationship with God. In our "protection" of the presence of God, by establishing a tradition to protect what we have discovered, we end up loosing His presence. Many times, traditions become stronger than the truth because once established they are easier to follow than it is for us to admit we have strayed from the Truth. In a Bible dictionary you will find that the word "traditional" means: to be habitually done, customary, time honored, set, fixed, routine, ritual, old, ancestral, handed down, and finally – long established belief. Some traditions are good, but many are not.

<u>Whether we believe and exhibit trust in the Word, our relationship, or our traditions, what we believe and what we value shows in how we live.</u>

(I do want to say that NO ONE is free from traditions. We make traditions instantly. We seem prone to starting a new one every day. So there is no condemnation to those who have fallen to the ones that restrict fellowship and communion in Christ). We simply need to be willing to see we have strayed from the place Jesus paid a high price for us to hold and be willing to return to HIM and lay down that which restrains or restricts us from the position we are to live.

The New Testament letters are the age of the church, our time. It is the time where "faith in God" and the foundational relationship between God and man is revealed afresh. It is a time of relational revelations, an exhibition of what it means to be a Christ-follower.

Here are some of the traditions that have been established in The Church to protect what we have received, that should be replaced with an openness to promote obedience to our relationship with Father, His Word and commands;

- "Come" to our church has replaced "GO" to the world.

- Sunday "worship" meetings has become the standard of "being in fellowship" instead of meeting together daily or weekly in common places or homes where intimate life happens, (small interactive gatherings).

- Clergy/laity division, instead of each member and joint supplying for the edifying of the body.

- Leaders "over" (world style of leadership) instead of servant leadership (Mt.20:25-28).

- "Church buildings" have replaced houses, and local community gatherings.

- Optional obedience to Christ's commands (a grace-grace mentality) has replaced commanded obedience – a place where honor, obedience, and sacrifice are embraced in order to fulfill Christ's commission to us.

- A powerless congregational style meeting of the Body of Christ. One without the naturally supernatural presence of The Love of God changing what cannot be changed by men. The Body should be naturally supernatural, not just a few leaders.

- One man in control, dictating Father's will, in charge of and over all that happens in our meetings, doing most of the teaching and preaching instead of 2-3 sharing in our gatherings and the involvement of the whole Body in our meetings. (*The Word actually never says to preach to the Church!*)

- Sitting has become the norm for 93% of the church, going should be, and we leaders are responsible for this statistic.

Once I got this new focus on relationship and fellowship with the Lord there had to be a tearing down of many of my previous practices, (dealing with traditions). As I submitted to what Father showed me was nothing but "man's traditions," Father began to implant, "*the need of the relationship*". **Relationships are only as strong as the communication or conversations involved in them.** The fellowship of the body is the same and also foundational to the cause of Christ. Whether it is fellowship with Father or His Body, *our conversation reveals the relationship.* Tradition has taught us that "fellowship of the brethren" is done in a building on Sunday mornings and maybe one or two other times a week at the direction of the "clergy" - and is restricted to what the leaders say is fellowship. That tradition has done much to destroy the true fellowship of the saints where all speak and interact together. **Fellowship is not a meeting, but a gathering!** The church began meeting in houses for the most part. There were a few big meetings, but predominately it is stated they met in houses. (See throughout the NT the references to the meetings held in a variety of people's houses). Thus, from the beginning of The Church we see the "fellowship of the saints" was in the community where they lived and in these homes, God moved!

In all the countries we minister in around the world, the great discipleship movements are found mostly in homes and through small groups meeting together and fellowshipping; experiencing

God's presence like at the beginning. These movements are not found in big buildings or groups.

Fellowship is relational conversations centered around common desires and beliefs. It is a friendship/relationship/family type communion of connected hearts.

The problem is that in any relationship, that is worth anything, there is humility and vulnerability to embrace, as well as chaos and disagreements to go through that have the potential to divide and destroy. In fellowship there is always a choice, whether to stay or walk away. Unfortunately, in Christianity we tend to look at our differences and "faults," magnifying them rather than looking "over" them like we do with our friends, and then we walk away from what should be family. Real fellowship is centered on diversity, tolerance and forgiveness, like all friendships and relationships.

Hebrews 10:23-25 (NKJV) Let us hold fast the confession of our hope without wavering, for He who promised is faithful. 24 And let us consider one another in order to stir up love and good works, 25 not forsaking the assembling of ourselves together, as is the manner of some, but exhorting one another, and so much the more as you see the Day approaching.

Assembling – to bring together or gather in one place, to put or fit together the parts, to come together, meet.

Fellowship happens in *a community bound together in conversation and life*: Fellowship is companionship, compatibility, forgiveness, sociability, comradeship, camaraderie, friendship, mutual support; togetherness, solidarity, informal intimacy.

Fellowship has the intonation of participating together. It is diversity walking together for a common goal. Real fellowship does not just tolerate diversity but cherishes it. In the traditional church setting, fellowship has come to mean; association, society, club, league, union, guild, affiliation, alliance, fraternity, sorority, benevolent society.

True Christian Fellowship has been greatly affected by all the traditions we have picked up over the generations. Our fellowship should be a sharing together, centered around the truth and not the traditions of men that restrict or circumvent Christ's desire and decrees for us. Generally speaking, real fellowship does not occur in traditional Church meetings, as participation is restricted to a few sharers and most present are restrained to the position of listeners.

In our homes, businesses, restaurants and coffee shops we tend to all contribute, thus we have an involvement in real fellowship. *Man's Church traditions including a clergy/laity division tend to keep people apart rather than bring them into community. They are formal, and restrictive by nature; thus, they avoid the intimacy amongst **all** necessary for Christ to be **all** He wants to be within His Church.* Fellowship is the foundation of relationship. The conversation determines the relationship, depth of fellowship and community. Church is to be community in action, doing the commands of God together.

Testimonies, singing, teachings, prayer, communion, and eating together are some of the principal ingredients of fellowship.

Christian fellowship also has God's presence in the midst of all that is going on - doing the impossible, changing lives!

The Elementary Principles of Christianity;

For several years there has been a question that I have asked many. The question is; "What are the basic or elementary principles of Christ?" What are the first things we should teach new believers? It is interesting that there have been few (whether pastor or believer) who can tell me what they are or where they can be found in the New Testament. **That is a bit bent!**

Jesus gives them to us in the 4 resurrection commands found in the Gospels. Paul gives us these elementary, first, foundation principles again in the book of Hebrews 5:12-6:2 .

**These foundational principles should be all believers'
starting point!** We will look at Paul's statements on this subject
first.

Heb 5:12 –Heb 6:3 (NKJV)

For though by this time you ought to be teachers, you need
someone to teach you again the first principles of the oracles of
God; and you have come to need milk and not solid food. For
everyone who partakes *only* of milk *is* unskilled in the word of
righteousness, for he is a babe. But solid food belongs to those
who are of full age, *that is,* those who by reason of use have their
senses exercised to discern both good and evil. [1]Therefore, leaving
the discussion of the elementary *principles* of Christ, let us go on to
perfection, not laying again the foundation of repentance from dead
works and of faith toward God, [2]of the doctrine of baptisms, of
laying on of hands, of resurrection of the dead, and of eternal
judgment. [3]And this we will do if God permits.

Hebrews 5 talks of who Jesus is, and in verse 11 Paul says
that there is much he cannot say as they - (the followers of Christ) -
have become "dull" or "hard of hearing." Then he explains to them
that they do not even know the "first principles of the oracles of
God," They are "unskilled," having not used or practiced these first
principles so that they could "discern" good (God) and evil (not
God).

In verses 1-3 of Chapter 6 Paul states, (verse 3) "if God
permits," they can go on from the elementary principles of Christ. In
the end of verse 1 and in verse 2 he defines the elementary or first
principles of Christ that they can go on from –*if God permits*.

Before I list these elementary principles, let us define; "first" (found in 5:12), and "elementary" (found in 6:1). Both words mean; a *commencement*, or (concrete) *chief* (in various applications of order, time, place or rank):—beginning, corner, (at the, the) first (estate), magistrate, power, principality, principle, rule.

"principle" (found in both places); something *orderly* in arrangement, that is, (by implication) a *serial* (*basal*, *fundamental*, *initial*) constituent (literally), proposition (figuratively): — element, principle, rudiment.

(in the AMPC translation of these scriptures there is this note added for clarification of the passage at the end of verse;

2; (AMPC) **These are all matters of which you should have been fully aware long, long ago**.*] (emphasis mine)*

From these definitions we can see that **these listed "foundational elements" should be the beginning,** *-- the first, chief rules or commands we, as believers, obey out of our desire to know God and walk with* Him. *They should be rudimentary, the very cornerstone in our living. If I am reading this passage correctly,* **until** *we are "practicing or using" these first principles we* **cannot** *go on to maturity. Actually, I think it would be safe to say that the practice or use of the elementary, first principles of Christ* **shows** *our maturity or lack of it. It is interesting to note that these principles that Paul lays out in 6:1-2 are found at the end of the four Gospels, and they are called, "the resurrection commands," spoken by Jesus and we will find that they are even mentioned in the Old Testament.*

But let's not get ahead of ourselves; before we can move on to 'perfection' we should "lay the foundation." Let's make a list of these first principles spoken of by Paul and put a bit of a definition to them.

- <u>Repentance from dead works</u> – turn from your way of living independent of God to following, committing and surrendering your life to Him.

- <u>Faith towards God</u>— exhibit, trust in, display relying on and living in adherence to Him

- <u>Doctrine of baptisms</u> (plural—more than one kind) – I will list 3: water, Spirit, and fire.

- <u>Laying on of hands</u> – this is anointing, and the miraculous, ie; "lay hands on the sick."

- <u>Resurrection of the dead</u> – no distinction thus probably both, raising the dead and being resurrected in the end. (*Although it does not say '**the'** resurrection, just resurrection*).

- <u>Eternal judgment</u> – **what we do will be judged.** Our "works of faith" are important and measurable. There is an end and "Grace, Grace" is not enough, our relationship must be lived. We are accountable and responsible to "show" our faith and position in Christ (sonship). We need to understand that we (our works of faith or lack thereof), will be judged in the end! (*This circles back around to the first part of this book where Jesus says, "get away from me, I do not know you"*). This is not taught in most traditional or non-traditional churches.

These **foundational** principles are where traditional Christianity (our legacy clergy/laity church system) and scriptural Christianity (living relationally and equally together in Jesus), divide. Walking in these basic or elementary commands is the place that reveals and fulfills our need to live out an intimate, naturally supernatural relationship with Christ. Our walk with Jesus can be measured and will be. The **elementary** principles need to be present in our living. (*The church has a hard time believing that these elementary principles need to be our foundation*)

Since these principles are **elementary**, disciples should be teaching disciples to "do" these **first.** And only after the "new" Christ-follower is doing these, and being naturally supernatural, should more be given. If we empower and loose new Christ followers into these **elementary** principles, they will not want to walk away or warm a pew. They will experience being needed and used by the Lord! Of course, to teach someone these basic Christian concepts, we ourselves will have to walk in these basic principles first. They must be demonstrated or modeled in us to be given away by us.

You cannot give away that which you do not possess.

To teach these principles you must first show Christ followers who they are, get them to understand the depth of "being saved." They need to know they are children of God, not slaves, and that intimacy with Father and Son is the goal and result of Christ's sacrifice. Jn.17:3. They also need to recognize the responsibility of the position they occupy as children of God. If Paul was the first to lay these elementary doctrines as the foundation for Christ followers to do, we might be able to say this is just his opinion of what should come first but He is not. Jesus left us with some commands after He was resurrected, and we need to compare these statements of Paul's with Jesus' last words to us from the Gospels.

All of Paul's writings must be put UNDER or in line with Jesus' commands to be interpreted correctly. To take Paul's writings and have them stand alone will lead you to some wrong ideas of what he is saying.

When put with Jesus' statements, many of Paul's words take a whole different slant to their meaning than what we have been taught.

In each of the four Gospels, Jesus leaves us with an "action" command after He was resurrected. His "last things" should be our "first things." (*In the beginning of His ministry He had His disciples laying hands on the sick, preaching, and baptizing. Then in the end, He emphasized to them again to continue to do and teach these things they had learned from the beginning to do*).

An Example of "last things, first things"

In living as a parent with young children, we begin to teach them important things first. For instance, if we have a wood stove, one of the first principles we teach our young children is not to touch the stove, as it will burn them. Second, we will teach them "do not play with matches." Then as they grow, we teach them how to take care of the stove and how to use matches safely. Why?

Because we know that these principles have the potential to keep us warm or destroy, not only their lives, but the whole family.

Years go by and we have taught our children many things but the first time we leave them alone in the house for an hour or two by themselves what do we re-iterate?" "Don't play with matches and be careful with the wood stove!" These "first things" could be called "elementary principles of living" in our family and house. If someone comes to our home with kids, they are told first thing, "That stove is hot and will burn you, so be careful around it. And do not play with the matches we use to start the fire as they can really do some damage to you, others and the house."

In the commission or resurrection commands, Jesus had His disciples begin the Church age with teaching others to do the things He trained them to do from the beginning. (He re-emphasizes the continued foundation and calling for all to walk in). Let's look at what Jesus left them to observe or do:

Mt 28:18 –Mt 28:20 (NKJV)

And Jesus came and spoke to them, saying, "All authority has been given to Me in heaven and on earth. Go therefore and make disciples of all the nations, baptizing them in the name of the Father and of the Son and of the Holy Spirit, teaching them to observe all things that I have commanded you; and lo, I am with you always, *even* to the end of the age." Amen.

Mk 16:15 –Mk 15:18

[15]And He said to them, "Go into all the world and preach the gospel to every creature. [16]He who believes and is baptized will be saved; but he who does not believe will be condemned.

[17]And these signs will follow those who believe: In My name they will cast out demons; they will speak with new tongues; [18]they will take up serpents; and if they drink anything deadly, it will by no means hurt them; they will lay hands on the sick, and they will recover."

Lk 24:46 –Lk 24:49 (NKJV)

Then He said to them, "Thus it is written, and thus it was necessary for the Christ to suffer and to rise from the dead the third day, and that repentance and remission of sins should be preached in His name to all nations, beginning at Jerusalem. And you are witnesses of these things. Behold, I send the Promise of My Father upon you; but tarry in the city of Jerusalem until you are endued with power from on high."

Jn 20:21 –Jn 20:23 (NKJV)

So Jesus said to them again, "Peace to you! As the Father has sent Me, I also send you." And when He had said this, He breathed on *them,* and said to them, "Receive the Holy Spirit. If you forgive the sins of any, they are forgiven them; if you retain the *sins* of any, they are retained."

In each of the above resurrection or commission commands we will find some, if not all, of the "first or elementary" principles of Christ listed by Paul in Heb.6:1-2.

In **Mt.28:18-20,** Jesus commissions and commands the disciples go make more disciples, to baptize, and teach these others to do what they themselves had been taught to do. If we look at what Jesus taught them "to do" or "observe", we find that basically He taught them to walk like He did. They preached repentance and faith toward God, laid hands on the sick, cast out demons, raised the dead… He had them do what Paul says are the basic principles of Christ and He told them to teach others to do these elementary principles. He also taught them to **be** God's naturally supernatural love and to live the characteristics of Father.

In **Mk 16:15-18,** Jesus commands His disciples to preach the gospel (repent and believe in Jesus), baptize, (in water and Spirit as these new believers are to speak in tongues, prophesy and be naturally supernatural creations).

The believers are also to do what the apostles or disciples did, cast out demons, lay hands on the sick, etc… Again, Jesus is having the disciples get others to do the same basic principles listed by Paul.

In **Lu 24:46-49,** Jesus speaks a little clearer (with more definition) through Luke. Basically, He tells them to teach repentance and remission of sins, and that they **should not** try to be a witness without "receiving power from on high" which according to Acts 1:4-8 is the baptism of the Spirit or the "Spirit coming **_upon_** them" with the purpose of giving them power to be a witness. (Laying on of hands, signs and wonders, healings, etc.). Ok, so here we have Jesus telling them to preach, and that they should do nothing without The POWER. Aren't these commission commands the same thing that Paul is saying in his list of the first or elementary principles of Christ: The doctrine of baptisms, laying on of hands, resurrection of the dead?

In **Jn 20:21-23,** Jesus makes it all real plain and simple. He uses few words in His statement to the disciples. **"I am sending you just like I was sent!"** That definitely is saying to do all that Paul describes in His elementary principles because Jesus models what He instructs us to live. In John's gospel is where it gets a bit interesting. To understand how we are sent, "just like Jesus was sent", we must look at Lu 4:18 and see Jesus' commission or how He was sent. **NOTE; Jesus was baptized in water and the Spirit "was on Him as He began His ministry."** Compare His commission to Paul's **basic elementary principles** that new believers should walk in, and the **resurrection commission - commands** Jesus had given the first disciples!

Lk 4:18 –Lk 4:19 (NKJV) "The Spirit of the Lord is **upon Me**"

Because He has anointed Me;

To preach the gospel to the poor;

He has sent Me to heal the brokenhearted,

To proclaim liberty to the captives

And recovery of sight to the blind,

To set at liberty those who are oppressed;

To proclaim the acceptable year of the Lord."

(*upon, not in, emphasis mine)

Is this not the same commission that we have in the resurrection commands and in Paul's elementary principles of Christ? *Jesus was sent to do these, to model what He wanted His disciples to do*, AND what He wanted them to teach others to model and do after He left to go be with Father!

Paul's version of the great commission;

2 Timothy 2:1-2 (NKJV) You therefore, my son, be strong in the grace that is in Christ Jesus. 2 And the things that you have heard from me among many witnesses, commit these to faithful men who will be able to teach others also.

How did we get to a place where we teach new followers of Christ to "sit" and NOT what is shown biblically to be the "basic," **rudimentary commands or principles of Christ – to GO** ?

My Lady Dana asks this question of a lot of people, "Why is it easier to believe a lie than the truth?" I think in this case it would be, "Why is it easier to follow the traditions of man rather than being obedient to the Word of God?"

Why do we justify not changing when we see the truth? Why is that acceptable behavior for us?

Discipleship/Intimacy;

We have been teaching discipleship/intimacy with God for many years in many countries and settings. When I am presenting the concept of Mt. 28:18-20 to leaders in the traditional church settings it is such a paradigm shift that after the training is over, many of the pastors or leaders will come to me and say, "We see that what you are saying is true, ***but*** we will continue to do what we have done as this discipleship could cost us too much, and it is too hard." They will say it will not be accepted by their denomination – or they will say that if they do it they will lose their "position" as pastor. **NOT ONE HAS EVER SAID to me that this teaching IS NOT SCRIPTURAL**, just the opposite, they know what has just been said is **The Truth,** but will not repent and follow what they admit is God. It is easier and more comfortable for them to do what they have always done; even though they know what they are doing doesn't work or change the communities they exist in. How insane is that? How BENT! These same leaders who will not change what they are doing, with fervor and tears flowing will get together and pray fervently that God will save the people in their communities.They will fast, pray and constantly bring in "new programs" and "anointed teachers or preachers" in hopes of seeing a move of God.

But, they will not repent nor change. Christ followers trust them to teach/model the TRUTH, so they do what their leaders do, rather than what is written; that is scary! If we leaders are unwilling to change when we get a further revelation of 'The Truth', why do we expect Father or Jesus to answer our prayers?

The same questions are always there. Why do we pray if we are unwilling to obey? Why do we refuse to acknowledge the error of our ways? Why do we read the Bible if we have already decided what it says in spite of what is written on its pages? (That might be a bit "bent".)

Why do we justify our powerless Gospel? And why do we reject the need of His presence and power found in biblical statements like Jesus saying; **"As the Father has sent me so I send you**!" (Jn.20:21) or Paul's statements in **1 Corinthians 2:4 and 4:20 NKJV, (2:4)** *"And my speech and my preaching were NOT with persuasive words of human wisdom but in demonstration of the Spirit and Power OF GOD."* **(4:20)***"for the kingdom of God is not in word but Power."*

We leaders must step down from our "position of authority." And become the servants of all. We must "empower and equip" the Church with the authority and "fullness of Christ." The elementary principles of Christ **must** be a part of **every** believer's foundation. … We leaders and all believers must go back to the *elementary principles of Christ* and live them, thus equipping others to do the same.

I find it interesting that in all the countries we go to, it is the traditional church, especially, that struggles with this imperative of ALL having Jesus presence and power the most.

That must speak to the broader universal struggle to truly trust and obey Jesus and live as He lived. What does it say about we who call ourselves believers when we so often reject Jesus' basic teachings and listen to the enemy; when we respect the traditions of men more often than we do His Word? Why do we do that? How broken God's heart must be.

One of the first times that I actually prayed what I heard from Father over someone; where I actually realized that I was responding to His voice and only speaking what I heard, happened on the last day of a series of meetings we did in a park. People had stayed away by the hundreds. All of our advertising on radio and with posters had not brought but a few. It was pretty disappointing from the standpoint of the size of the crowds at that time of my walk with Jesus. On the final day there was maybe 15 people present. On this day, a couple of young Native Americans brought their mother to the park carrying her from the car to a rock near where we were set up. They listened to the preaching and music, but never joined in. When we had given the altar call, that no one responded to, we began to pack our equipment up to leave. One of the young men finally came over to me and very quietly asked if we would pray for his mother. Responding that we would, I gathered our team and went over to this rock she had been placed on by her sons. She had crippling arthritis and looked a lot like a pretzel sitting where they had placed her on this flat rock. Her back was so bent that she could only see down. Her legs and arms were immobilized by being out of joint.

Her hands were all crooked. I felt like crying the moment I got close enough to see how bad she was crippled. I did not know what to do. I had just preached of a miraculous God, but I was actually without much faith at the moment that God could do much with her. The only way to speak to her was for me to lay down on the ground by the rock and look up at her face. Doing this, I asked her why she had come. She told me that she had heard of our meeting on the radio and that God had spoken to her that if she came and I prayed for her she would be healed. She had come from a town about 50 miles from the park where we were meeting. I related to the others gathered what her request was for, and we began to pray. We prayed every scripture we knew about healing, anointed her with oil, and spoke all the words I had ever heard prayed over anyone before. Nothing happened! As I laid back down on the ground to talk with her after our 15-minute scriptural, religious prayer, and as I was looking up into her eyes, the Lord spoke so clearly to my heart, "Tell her that when she forgives the man who abused her youngest son 19 years before that I will heal her." I told her, saw tears well up in her eyes and got up off the ground. I had no more I could say, I smiled at her boys, told them I was through and we began to walk away. I turned around after a few steps and watched as her sons picked her gently from the rock and carried her back to their car, put her in and then drove off.

The truth - I never expected to see her again! I can't say I expected her to be healed, either. That may sound a bit callous but is not meant to be. I just had nothing else I could do for her and doubted that what I had done would change anything for her.

The story continues about 3 months later in another town where I am speaking at a 3-day event. I was not to speak until the last day so I was attending the meetings, visiting with people, praying over people and sharing the Gospel at every opportunity.

I noticed from the first meeting that there was this Native American lady who seemed to always be close to wherever I was. She did not speak to me, but I knew she was following me. By the second day I was aware that in every meeting she was seated directly behind me. It was bothering me some, but I did not ask her why or talk with her. On the third day, I was to speak during the main meeting. I had been asked to share my testimony of Christ. I was seated in the third row, as I remember, and in that meeting this Indian lady was seated behind me. When I would turn and look at her, she would smile and move her hands around a bit. When I was called to come up and speak, I was in the midst of being deeply troubled by this lady. As I turned to the crowd and began to speak The Lord gave me a nudge, "Don't you remember her? I told you she would be healed!" It took about 5 minutes before the answer hit me and I stopped speaking and began crying. As I looked up at her again, she smiled once more while raising her hands moved them around, clenched her hands into fists then opened them again palms up. I am not sure why but at that moment the Lord began moving mightily in this meeting and people everywhere began to cry and shout. I left the stage area without another word and walked to this Indian lady and sat down. Quietly, she told me the rest of the story - she had her boys drive her from the meeting in the park, 3 months before, to the house of the man who had abused her youngest son 19 years before.

Her sons carried her to his door and when he opened it she told him, "I forgive you for abusing my son 19 years ago!" Her sons then took her back to the car, drove her home and put her in bed as she could not do anything by herself. The next morning she had gotten up and cooked her sons breakfast – **totally healed!** She was very quiet and we did not talk much more,

but she thanked me for the prayer I had prayed that day and the words that had brought her healing and health. I found out that to get to the meetings we were at she was walking over a mile each day. Hallelujah! This experience taught me some new things about trust and not dismissing the Living Word. Even when we are doubting, obedience to the Voice and Love of Father looses His presence. All of our scripture quoting, while we were praying for her in the park, was not the key to her healing, but the key was to trust to obey His voice and to speak what He said she needed to do to receive her healing. Jesus has told us that, "the words that I speak to you, I do not speak on my own authority, but the Father who dwells in Me does the works." Jn 14:10 That is why we will do the works that Jesus did and greater...vs.12. _If we want to see what Jesus saw, then we must also speak what we hear The Spirit speak and recognize,_ **it is the Father who does the works ALWAYS.** Through the years, this example Father had me experience has strengthened me many times to simply trust and obey The Spirit of God and speak what I hear Him say in my heart.

The re-vamping of "the desire of my heart";

A few years after the previous shared event happened in my life, I was sitting in my house one day praying, asking Father to give me the desires of my heart. In some ways I was actually demanding that He give me the desire of my heart as I had been taught that was how we should hold God to His promises, "You promised to give me the desires of my heart Father so I remind you of your word! Give me my desires!"

At this time I was very much into the "faith movement" of the 80s and was Charismatic to the hilt. I had been taught that if God does not move, then move God! *(I have figured out since then that commanding God may be a bad move. Reminding Him of something He has said is acceptable when in intimacy with Him and with the right attitude, but we should be **very** careful. Satan wanted to be in command over what God had created, his arrogance was not received well — hell may not be the best place to end up)*

Anyway, back to that day when I was sitting praying. As I was speaking, I was suddenly caught up in a vision. I found myself in our kitchen doing dishes and cleaning up when there was a knock on the kitchen door. I looked up to see Jesus standing there. Opening the door I asked Him why He was there? "Neil, I would like to give you the desire of your heart today. It is just across town and if you would take a walk with me we will go get it." Our town was fairly small and in an hour you could easily walk across it. So I replied to Him, "Sure, but I promised Dana I would be home to receive the boys after school at 3 pm so I need to be back by then. I need to keep my word to her." It was about 10 am and He told me that was not a problem. I grabbed a jacket and my cap and we left the house. It was a beautiful day and as we walked we were sharing about the weather and the squirrels running around, etc. As we approached a street corner Jesus stopped me and asked if it would be OK if we asked a couple of other guys if they wanted to come with us and get the desires of their hearts, also. I shrugged my shoulders and mumbled, "Sure why not." We stopped at this house where two guys were praying together, and Jesus asked them if they wanted to see the desire of their hearts fulfilled that day? Both were excited and agreed to walk with us across town to get the desire of their hearts fulfilled! As we walked down the street Jesus stopped us and mentioned this lady that had been asking Him to stop by for a visit and He wondered if it would be ok to stop. One of the other guys asked how long it would take because this walk was supposed to be about getting **"our"** desires fulfilled. Jesus promised it would not take too long and it was not very much farther to the place where we would get our hearts' desires fulfilled.

As we got to the house the other two guys chose to stay outside. The house was pretty run down and there was some weeds in the yard. I went in with Jesus and stood inside the door as Jesus went over to this older lady and put His hand on her head. He was speaking softly to her, then stopped and looking at me, asked if I would go into her kitchen and see what was in her cupboards.

I nodded and left the room and went to the kitchen. I could not find any food in the whole place. I came back, walked up to Jesus standing by this lady with His hand on her and shared my findings. He left her for a moment and taking me aside asked if I had any money and would I go down to the neighborhood store and pick up a few things for her? I had a twenty in my pocket and told Him I would go. He emphasized that as soon as I got back we could go on. Outside, when I told the two men what I was about to do they got pretty mad. They told me that this walk was to be about fulfilling the desires of their heart, not stopping at some rundown house and then being sent to get some groceries for some smelly, old lady. They had other things to do and needed to get moving. When I returned in a few minutes, and finished unloading the food items, Jesus said we could go. As we left, the two guys complained a bit to Jesus and asked if we were going to get our desires or not.

Jesus said that it would not be long and they would receive what they were asking for. So we continued a block or two more and once more Jesus stopped us and asked if we could visit this family who had just received Him as their Lord. He said He just wanted to encourage them and it would only take a few minutes.

I looked at my watch and it was about 12:30 so I was good, but the other two said that they had some important things to do and we needed to be quick about it. They did not have any time to waste. When we entered the house there were 3 kids and the husband and wife gathered in the living room reading scripture together. When Jesus joined them, the kids got up and came over where I was standing with the other guys and began to ask questions about Jesus. They wanted us to tell them some testimonies.

The other two went over and sat down on the couch and just looked at Jesus with unhappy faces. So I took the kids into another room and answered questions and told them stories of my walk with Jesus. Jesus had the husband and wife in tears of joy as He sat with them. The look on their faces was very moving and I was touched by what I saw. In a short time Jesus told me it was time to go so I hugged the kids and said good bye to the couple who were still in tears of joy over the visit. As we left the two guys were quite indignant with Jesus and had made up their minds to leave and go back home as they did not have time to wander around aimlessly. They had some important appointment they had forgotten so they left us. Jesus looked a bit sad at their exit but turned and suggested that we get started onward. I was finding this walk interesting but also was getting a bit anxious about the time as I had promised Dana I would be home for the kids. Jesus told me that He would get me home in time to keep my promise. He showed me up ahead the building that contained the promised desire of my heart. It was just a couple of blocks away. I was excited! About halfway down the first block Jesus stopped and looked at me with such warmth that I almost melted.

He asked once more, "There is one more place I would like to stop, would it be ok?... we are so close, and it will not take long. It is just a couple of young people, maybe 10 minutes, no more. Will that be ok?" Looking at my watch and knowing how long it would take to get home I said with a bit of a reluctant tone, "Ok, Jesus but then we have got to go!" "Absolutely, we will have no more detours," was His reply. When we entered the building there was more than a couple of young people, but it was still a small group. They were sitting on the floor singing and writing on pads on the floor before them. Jesus was smiling and just stood inside the room with me at first.

The young people were singing songs I had never heard before and I realized that they were writing new love songs to Jesus! For a few minutes we just stood there. Then Jesus went over and stood in the midst of them and raising His arms began to radiate light all around Him as they sang. Pretty soon we all were crying in joy and His love just permeated everything. After a bit I realized that I would have to leave soon or miss the desire of my heart. I looked at Jesus and He turned and came to where I was standing. He said quietly, "We need to leave now if we are to get you the desire of your heart." He said it with such a smile I was undone at His love. Then He looked back at the young people worshiping Him with some new songs and we both breathed deeply of the fragrance in the room. As we left the building I was overcome with a thought, "What was the desire of my heart?" Walking down the street I got it! I knew! I turned and looking at Jesus   whispered, "Jesus, if it is ok I think I better get home before the boys get there and fix them a snack. Maybe tomorrow we could take another walk if you wanted to!" "I would love to," was His response.

At our house we hugged, and He walked off. For many years, the desire of my heart that I kept asking Him to fulfill, was that I would know Him and know His heart. I wanted to walk with Him and watch Him Love people... No amount of "ministry" would ever do! At that moment I had realized that if I was walking with Him, that **WAS** the desire of my heart and that would be enough! *I quit praying for "my" desire that day and started praying that I would fulfill "His" desire!*

WE have walked many miles together since that day, some delightful and some sad, but I always look forward to another day to live close, walking with Him. His love is amazing and wherever He wants to go, I am good with that. It will be enough!

May Father bless all you put your hand to do!   In Father's Hand, neil

Separate thought: Why is it so hard for men to choose

to follow God and pursue relationship?

What does our current condition say about mankind

and what does our Christian

walk say about who God is?

Our conversation is the relationship;

The foundation that we build on determines what we will get out of our relationship with Father. Our identity in Him, our perspective and the position we see ourselves in with the world, will affect all we hear, and live. If we build on a true desire to find God, and to know Him, we are off to a great start. Our hunger for Him dictates how much we will **Know him and be known by Him**.

Knowing Him is a lifetime mission. We can't think that we will become an amazing person of God that has true intimacy with Him, without truly showing our trust in Him and living in pursuit of a close, personal, dynamic, realistic fellowship and relationship with Him. That is what it takes for us to experience all He is and we are. We need to be like Jesus and die to self, live to fulfill Father's heart, desire and thus live for others. We need to live in ways to be found in God at all times. When we commit to "knowing Father and

Jesus," we are investing in Eternity. Discipleship is at times a hard pill to swallow, but if we do not give away what we have received and then cause them to give it away, we do not have much. Discipleship is part of dying to ourselves and our own ideas of what being a true follower of Jesus really is.

It illustrates the true Power of Choice. All of creation and Mankind's future hangs on the power of our choice. From the fall in the garden, to this present day, each day will be affected by the reality of our choices! Picking up our cross daily to follow Jesus is **Our choice, and will affect the future, because God our Father is true love and thus will always honor choice...**

A change in identity, perspective and position is needed by all who call Jesus Lord. Wrath is not who God is, it is the result of man's choice and Father's great love for all He created. Wrath breaks Father's heart, "He takes no pleasure in the death of the wicked"! Our identity changes when we have the right identity of God, (Father, Son, and Holy Spirit)! HE IS LOVE; He will not change and become evil. He will always give us choice - our choice will dictate what the results of our living will be. *Jesus came to save, restore, and redeem - thus destroying the "works" of the enemy.* The refusal to accept truth, love and grace will produce wars, death, and destruction. But it is not God's nature or desire to destroy!

"Now that you know how God designed our relationship to truly be; how will you start on your journey…". I think a lot of people want what I am finding, but don't know what to do to get it. I have given some of the steps I have taken and prayers I have prayed. It will take Honor, Obedience and sacrifice to Father! I

started with hunger and a prayer. I studied Him and His Word. Then I quit studying scripture to find eternal life and began to look for Jesus in the Word, JN. 5:39. In the midst of that I would pray from my heart, asking God to make His and Jesus' presence real in my life. As time went on, I can look back and see how God has answered my prayers, and truly taught me how scripture and relationship applied in my life. I made my commitment to following him, something that NOTHING can destroy.

I chose to follow Him because He is God! - NOT because of His promises. *(Though they be "yea and amen")*

I am always about reality and having something tangible that others could see and do. I'm sure Jesus is no respecter of persons! The Word says Paul is "the least of the saints" so whatever Father did with and for Paul should be a foundation for us all to start from.

What we believe to be true will never change The Truth, but, and, if we would be willing to look afresh at the Truth and accept it, the truth, will change us. WE can be whom Father has created us to be...

We need to begin to be "BENT Letters" that reveal the Lord and not the traditions of men, nor the ways of the world.

Thanks for taking the time to ponder my writing. It is a blessing to walk with Him and His body of believers!

As my friends know, "will write more later,"

In Father's Hand, neil

Made in the USA
Middletown, DE
06 December 2022

17287135R00064